D1210006

Payroll
Best Practices

Payroll
Best Practices

Steven M. Bragg

John Wiley & Sons, Inc.

For general information on our other products and services, or technical support,
please contact our Customer Care Department within the United States at 800-762-
2974, outside the United States at 317-572-3993 or fax 317-572-4002.

Wiley also publishes its books in a variety of electronic formats. Some content that
appears in print may not be available in electronic books.

For more information about Wiley products, visit our Web site at *www.wiley.com*.

Library of Congress Cataloging-in-Publication Data:

Bragg, Steven M.
  Payroll best practices / Steven M. Bragg
    p. cm.
  Includes index.
  ISBN-13 978-0-471-70226-9
  ISBN-10 0-471-70226-9 (cloth)
  1. Payrolls—Management. 2. Wages—Accounting. I. Title.
  HG4028.P5B73 2005
  658.3′21—dc22

                                              2005000044

Printed in the United States of America

10 9 8 7 6 5 4 3 2 1

To Clint, who tolerated his odd roommate all those years ago.
Imagine living with an accounting major!
Sort of like keeping a troll in the shoe closet?

About the Author

Steven Bragg, CPA, CMA, CIA, CPIM, has been the chief financial officer or controller of four companies, as well as a consulting manager at Ernst & Young and auditor at Deloitte & Touche. He received a master's degree in finance from Bentley College, an MBA from Babson College, and a bachelor's degree in Economics from the University of Maine. He has been the two-time president of the Colorado Mountain Club, is an avid alpine skier and mountain biker, and is a certified master diver. Mr. Bragg resides in Centennial, Colorado. He has published the following books through John Wiley & Sons:

Accounting and Finance for Your Small Business

Accounting Best Practices

Accounting for Payroll

Billing and Collections Best Practices

Business Ratios and Formulas

The Controller's First Years

The Controller's Function

Controller's Guide to Costing

Controller's Guide to Planning and Controlling Operations

Controllership

Cost Accounting

Design and Maintenance of Accounting Manuals

Essentials of Payroll

Fast Close

Financial Analysis

GAAP Implementation Guide

Inventory Accounting

Inventory Best Practices

Just-in-Time Accounting

Managing Explosive Corporate Growth
The New CFO Financial Leadership Manual
Outsourcing
Payroll Best Practices
Sales and Operations for Your Small Business
The Ultimate Accountants' Reference

Also:

Advanced Accounting Systems (Institute of Internal Auditors)
Run the Rockies (CMC Press)

Contents

Preface

This book contains more than 120 best practices related to every phase of a company's payroll activities: tracking employee time, recording deductions, paying employees, calculating commissions, outsourcing, control systems, and more. It also shows how to integrate these best practices into the existing payroll system, with an entire chapter devoted to detailed policies and procedures that incorporate best practices. There is even a recommended implementation plan for achieving the greatest efficiency improvement through the selective use of payroll best practices. An appendix summarizes the best practices presented. The glossary contains a dictionary of relevant terms. In short, this volume is the go-to source for payroll improvements.

Chapter 2 covers a number of ways to automate the timekeeping process or at least to simplify it, while Chapter 3 presents methods to reduce employee deductions and convert to automation through the use of employee and manager self-service. Chapter 4 describes a number of forms and reports, as well as advanced forms of data storage and electronic presentation. Chapter 5 shows how to convert to a variety of electronic employee payments as well as ways to encourage employees to accept the change. Chapter 6 contains a broad range of methods designed to simplify the calculation of commissions, while Chapter 7 addresses the increasingly popular approach of outsourcing multiple payroll functions. Chapter 8 describes many management-related payroll tasks, including training, process improvement, and customer service issues. Chapter 9 covers how to use major computer systems to improve payroll processing, while Chapter 10 addresses a number of key controls over the payroll area. Chapter 11 describes several payroll-specific measurements that are of use in designing a payroll metrics tracking system. Chapter 12 includes a broad array of policies and procedures designed to support the best practices noted earlier in the book, while Chapter 13 presents a simplified best practices implementation plan. The appendix contains a summary of all the best practices in the book, and the glossary contains key payroll-related terminology.

Finally, one does not install a best practice merely by ordering that it be done. The "Make it so!" approach of Captain Picard of the USS *Enterprise* does not always work. Instead, read Chapter 1, "Success or Failure with Best Practices," to learn what factors will impact a best practices implementation and how to increase the odds of success.

The best practice description in each chapter is followed by graphics indicating the cost and implementation duration for each item. A single stack of dollar bills represents an inexpensive best practice; two or three stacks represent increasing levels of expense. Similarly, one clock represents a minimal implementation interval, while two or three clocks indicate increasingly lengthy periods before a best practice is likely to be completed.

Use this book to improve all aspects of the payroll department's processes to increase efficiency, lower error rates, and increase service to employees. Doing this can result in a significant reduction in staffing needs within the payroll department, while also transitioning it from primarily data-entry tasks to a more analytical systems orientation.

The foundation for this book is the author's *Accounting Best Practices*, which is now in its third edition. That book contains approximately 30 payroll best practices, all of which can be found in this book. However, this book provides more than 90 additional best practices, giving the reader a much more in-depth knowledge of how this critical functional area can be improved. For a general view of best practices covering the entire accounting function, read the author's *Accounting Best Practices*; for a detailed view of inventory issues, try *Inventory Best Practices*, which includes almost 200 more best practices. Finally, *Billing and Collections Best Practices*, with yet another 200-plus best practices, is perfect for those trying to reduce bad debts or accelerate cash flow in the receivables area.

Steven M. Bragg
Centennial, Colorado
June 2005

1

Success or Failure with Best Practices[*]

This chapter is about implementing best practices. It begins by describing those situations where best practices are most likely to be installed successfully. The key components of a successful best practice installation are also noted, as well as how to duplicate best practices throughout an organization. When planning to add a best practice, it is also useful to know the ways in which the implementation can fail, so the chapter provides a lengthy list of reasons for failure. Only by carefully considering all of these issues in advance can one hope to achieve a successful best practice implementation that will result in increased levels of efficiency.

1.1 The Most Fertile Ground for Best Practices

Before installing any best practice, it is useful to review the existing environment to see if there is a reasonable chance for the implementation to succeed. These points note the best environments in which best practices can be installed and have a fair chance of continuing to succeed:

- *If benchmarking shows a problem.* Some organizations regularly compare their performance levels against those of other companies, especially those with a reputation for having extremely high levels of performance. A significant difference in the performance levels of these other organizations and the company doing the benchmarking can serve

---

[*]Adapted with permission from Chapter 2 of Steven M. Bragg, *Accounting Best Practices, Third Edition* (Hoboken, NJ: John Wiley & Sons, 2003).

as a reminder that continuous change is necessary in order to survive. If management sees and heeds this warning, the environment in which best practices will be accepted is greatly improved.

- *If management has a change orientation.* Some managers have a seemingly genetic disposition toward change. If a department has such a person in charge, there will certainly be a drive toward many changes. If anything, this type of person can go too far, implementing too many projects with not enough preparation, resulting in a confused operations group whose newly revised systems may take a considerable amount of time to untangle. The presence of a detail-oriented second-in-command is very helpful for preserving order and channeling the energies of such a manager into the most productive directions.

- *If the company is experiencing poor financial results.* A significant loss, or a trend in that direction, serves as a wake-up call to management, which in turn results in the creation of a multitude of best practices projects. In this case, the situation may even go too far, with so many improvement projects going on at once that there are not enough resources to go around. The result may be the ultimate completion of few, if any, of the best practices.

- *If there is new management.* Most people who are newly installed as managers want to make changes in order to leave their marks on the organization. Although this can involve less effective best practice items such as organizational changes or a new strategic direction, it is possible that there will be a renewed focus on efficiency that will result in the implementation of new best practices.

In short, as long as there is willingness by management to change and a good reason for doing so, then there is fertile ground for the implementation of a multitude of best practices.

1.2 Implementing Best Practices

The implementation of any best practice requires a great deal of careful planning. However, planning is not enough. The implementation process itself requires a number of key components to ensure a successful conclusion. This section discusses those components.

One of the first implementation steps for all but the simplest best practice improvements is to *study and flowchart the existing system* about to be improved. By doing so, one can ascertain any unusual requirements that are not readily apparent and that must be included in the planning for the upcoming implementation. Although some reengineering efforts do not spend much time on this task, on the grounds that the entire system is about to be replaced, the same issue still applies—there are usually special requirements, unique to any company, that must be addressed in a new system. Accordingly, nearly all implementation projects must include this critical step.

Another issue is the *cost-benefit analysis*. This is a compilation of all the costs required to both install and maintain a best practice, which is offset against the benefits of doing so. These costs must include project team payroll and related expenses, outside services, programming costs, training, travel, and capital expenditures. This step is worth a great deal of attention, for a wise manager will not undertake a new project, no matter how cutting edge and high profile it may be, if there is not a sound analysis in place that clearly shows the benefit of moving forward with it.

Yet another implementation issue is the *use of new technology*. Although there may be new devices or software on the market that can clearly improve the efficiency of a company's operations, and perhaps even make a demonstrative impact on a company's competitive situation, it still may be more prudent to wait until the technology has been tested in the marketplace for a short time before proceeding with an implementation. This is a particular problem if only one supplier offers the technology, especially if that supplier is a small one or has inadequate funding, with the attendant risk of going out of business. In most cases, the prudent manager will elect to use technology that has proven itself in the marketplace rather than using the most cutting-edge applications.

Of great importance to many best practice implementations is *system testing*. Any new application, unless it is astoundingly simple, carries with it the risk of failure. This risk must be tested repeatedly to ensure that it will not occur under actual use. The type of testing can take a variety of forms. One is volume testing, to ensure that a large number of employees using the system at the same time will not result in failure. Another is feature testing, in which sample transactions that test the boundaries of the possible information to be used are run through the system. Yet another possibility is recovery testing—bringing down a computer system suddenly to see how easy it is to restart. All of these approaches, or others, depending on the type of best practice, should be completed before unleashing a new application on employees.

One of the last implementation steps before firing up a new best practice is to *provide training* to employees in how to run the new system. This must be done as late as possible, because employee retention of this information will dwindle rapidly if not reinforced by actual practice. In addition, this training should be hands-on whenever possible, because employees retain the most information when training is conducted in this manner. It is important to identify in advance all possible users of a new system for training, since a few untrained employees can result in the failure of a new best practice.

A key element of any training class is procedures. These must be completed, reviewed, and made available for employee use not only at the time of training, but also at all times thereafter. A good manager must oversee the procedure creation and distribution phases. Procedure writing is a special skill that may require the hiring of technical writers, interviewers, and systems analysts to ensure that procedures are properly crafted. The input of users into the accuracy of all procedures is also an integral step in this process.

Even after the new system has been installed, it is necessary to conduct a *postimplementation review*. This analysis determines if the cost savings or efficiency improvements are in the expected range, what problems arose during the implementation that should be avoided during future projects, and what issues are still unresolved from the current implementation. This last point is particularly important, for many managers do not follow through completely on all stray implementation issues that inevitably arise after a new system is put in place. Only by carefully listing these issues and working through them will the employees using the new system be completely satisfied with how a best practice has been installed.

An issue that arises during all phases of a project implementation is *communications*. There may be a wide range of activities going on, and many will be dependent on each other; it is important that the status of all project steps be communicated to the entire project team, as well as all affected employees, continually. By doing so, a project manager can avoid such gaffes as having one task proceed without knowing that, due to changes elsewhere in the project, the entire task has been rendered unnecessary. These communications should not just be limited to project plan updates, but should include all meeting minutes in which changes are decided on, documented, and approved by team leaders. If this important item is paid attention to at every step of an implementation, the entire process will be completed much more smoothly.

As described in this section, a successful best practice implementation nearly always includes a review of the current system, a cost-benefit analysis, responsible use of new technology, system testing, training, and a postimplementation review, with a generous dash of communications at every step.

1.3 How to Use Best Practices: Best Practice Duplication

Duplicating a successful best practice when opening a new company facility, especially if expansion is contemplated in many locations over a short time period, can be a particularly difficult challenge. The difficulty with best practice duplication is that employees in the new locations typically are given a brief overview of a best practice and told to "go do it." Under this scenario, they only have a sketchy idea of what they are supposed to do, and so create a process that varies in some key details from the baseline situation. To make matters worse, managers at the new location may feel that they can create a better best practice from the start, and so create something that differs in key respects from the baseline. For both reasons, the incidence of best practice duplication failure is high.

To avoid these problems, a company should first be certain that it has accumulated all possible knowledge about a functioning best practice—the forms, policies, procedures, equipment, and special knowledge required to make it work properly—and then transfer this information into a concise document that can be shared with new locations. Second, a roving team of expert users must be commissioned to visit all new company locations and personally install the new systems, thereby ensuring that the proper level of experience with a best practice is brought to bear on a duplication activity. Finally, a company should transfer the practitioners of best practices to new locations on a semipermanent basis to ensure that the necessary knowledge required to make a best practice effective over the long term remains on site. By taking these steps, a company can increase its odds of spreading best practices throughout all of its locations.

A special issue is the tendency of a new company location to attempt to enhance a copied best practice at the earliest opportunity. This tendency frequently arises from the belief that one can always improve upon something that was created elsewhere. However, these changes may negatively impact other parts of the company's systems, resulting in an overall reduction in performance. Consequently, it is better to insist that new locations duplicate a best practice in all respects and use it to match the performance levels of the baseline location before they are allowed to make any changes to it. By doing so, the new location must take the time to fully utilize the best practice and learn its intricacies before they can modify it.

1.4 Why Best Practices Fail

There is a lengthy list of reasons why a best practice installation may not succeed, as noted in the following points. The various reasons for failure can be grouped into a relatively small cluster of primary reasons. The first is the lack of planning, which can include inadequate budgeting for time, money, or personnel. Another is the lack of cooperation by other entities, such as the programming staff or other departments that will be impacted by any changes. The final, and most important, problem is that there is little or no effort made to prepare the organization for change. This last item tends to build up over time as a multitude of best practices are implemented, eventually resulting in the total resistance by the organization to any further change. At its root, this problem involves a fundamental lack of communication, especially to those people who are most impacted by change. The completion of a single implementation without informing all employees of the change may be tolerated, but a continuous stream of changes will encourage a revolt. In alphabetical order, the various causes of failure are:

- *Alterations to packaged software.* A very common cause of failure is that a best practice requires changes to a software package provided by a software supplier; after the changes are made, the company finds that the newest release of the software contains features that it must have and so it updates the software—wiping out the programming changes that were made to accommodate the best practice. This problem can arise even if there is only a custom interface between the packaged software and some other application needed for a best practice, because a software upgrade may alter the data accessed through the interface. Thus, alterations to packaged software are doomed to failure unless there is absolutely no way that the company will ever update the software package.

- *Custom programming.* A major cause of implementation failure is that the programming required to make it a reality does not have the requested specifications, costs more than expected, arrives too late, is unreliable—or all of the above. Because many best practices are closely linked to the latest advances in technology, this is an increasingly common cause of failure. To keep from being a victim of programming problems, one should never attempt to implement the most "bleeding-edge" technology, because it is the most subject to failure. Instead, one should wait for some other company to work out all of the bugs and make it a reliable concept, and then proceed with the implementation. Also, it is useful to interview other people who have gone through a complete installation to see what tips they can give that will result in a smoother implementation. Finally, one always should interview any other employees who have had programming work done for them by the in-house staff. If the results of these previous efforts were not acceptable, it may be better to look outside the company for more competent programming assistance.

- *Inadequate preparation of the organization.* Communication is the key to a successful implementation. Lack of communication keeps an organization from understanding what is happening; this increases the rumors about a project, builds resistance to it, and reduces the level of cooperation that people are likely to give it. Avoiding this issue requires a considerable amount of up-front communication about the intents and likely impact of any project. That communication should target not just the impacted managers, but also all impacted employees, and to some extent even the corporation or department as a whole.

- *Intransigent personnel.* A major cause of failure is the employee who either refuses to use a best practice or actively tries to sabotage it. This type of person may have a vested interest in using the old system, does not like change in general, or has a personality clash with someone on the implementation team. In any of these cases, the person must be won over through good communication (especially if the employee is in a controlling position) or removed to a position that has no impact on the project. If neither of these actions is successful, the project will almost certainly fail.

- *Lack of control points.* One of the best ways to maintain control over any project is to set up regular review meetings, as well as additional meetings to review the situation when preset milestone targets are reached. These meetings are designed to see how a project is progressing, to discuss any problems that have occurred or are anticipated, and to determine how current or potential problems can best be avoided. Without the benefit of these regular meetings, it is much more likely that unexpected problems will arise or that existing ones will be exacerbated.

- *Lack of funding.* A project can be cancelled either because it has a significant cost overrun exceeding the original funding request or because it was initiated without any funding request in the first place. Either approach results in failure. Besides the obvious platitude of "Don't go over budget," the best way to avoid this problem is to build a cushion into the original funding request that should see the project through, barring any unusually large extra expenditures.

- *Lack of planning.* A critical aspect of any project is the planning that goes into it. If there is no plan, there is no way to determine the cost, number of employees, or time requirements, nor is there any formal review of the inherent project risks. Without this formal planning process, a project is very likely to hit a snag or be stopped cold at some point prior to its timely completion. Using proper planning results in a smooth implementation process that builds a good reputation for the project manager and thereby leads to more funding for additional projects.

- *Lack of postimplementation review.* Although a postimplementation review is not a criterion for the successful implementation of any single project, a missing review can cause the failure of later projects. For example, if such a review reveals that a project was completed despite the inadequate project planning skills of a specific manager, it might be best to use a different person in the future for new projects, thereby increasing the project's chances of success.

- *Lack of success in earlier efforts.* If a manager builds a reputation for not completing best practices projects successfully, it becomes increasingly difficult to complete new ones. The problem is that no one believes a new effort will succeed and so there is little commitment to doing it. Also, upper management is much less willing to allocate funds to a manager who has not developed a proven track record for successful implementations. The best way out of this jam is to assign a different manager to an implementation project, one with a proven track record of success.

- *Lack of testing.* A major problem for the implementation of especially large and complex projects, especially those involving programming, is that they are rushed into production without a thorough testing process to discover and correct all bugs that might interfere with or freeze the orderly conduct of work in the areas they are designed to improve. There is nothing more dangerous than to install a wonderful new system in a critical area of the company, only to see that critical function fail completely due to a problem that could have been discovered in a proper testing program. It is always worthwhile to build some extra time into a project budget for an adequate amount of testing.

- *Lack of top management support.* If a project requires a large amount of funding or the cooperation of multiple departments, it is critical to have the complete support of the top management team. If not, any required funding may not be allocated; there is also a strong possibility that any objecting departments will be able to sidetrack the project easily. This is an especially common problem when a project has no clear project sponsor at all—without a senior-level manager to drive it, a project will sputter along and eventually fade away without coming anywhere near completion.

- *Relying on other departments.* As soon as another department's cooperation becomes a necessary component of a best practice installation, the chances of success drop markedly. The odds of success become even smaller if multiple departments are involved. The main reason why this is true is the involvement of an extra manager, who may not have as much commitment to making the implementation a success. In addition, the staff of the other department may influence their manager not to help out, or the other department may not have a sufficient amount of funding to complete its share of the work. For example, the payroll staff could benefit greatly from merging the payroll and human resources (HR) databases in order to gain access to potentially more accurate employee address information in the HR database. However, this will not happen unless the HR department sees a sufficient need to fully support the merger.

- *Too many changes in a short time.* An organization will rebel against too much change if it is clustered into a short time frame. This rebellion will occur because change is unsettling, especially when it involves a large part of people's job descriptions, so that nearly everything they do is altered. Such large changes can result in direct employee resistance to further change, sabotaging new projects, a work slowdown, or (quite likely) the departure of the most disgruntled workers. This problem is best solved by planning for lapses between implementation projects to let employees settle down. The best way to accomplish this lag between changes without really slowing down the overall schedule of implementation is to shift projects around within the department, so that no functional area is on the receiving end of two consecutive projects.

The aim of listing all of these causes of failure is not to discourage the reader from attempting a best practice installation. Knowledge of possible problems allows one to prepare for and avoid all roadblocks on the path to ultimate implementation success.

1.5 Summary

This chapter has given an overview of the situations in which best practices implementations are most likely to succeed, what factors are most important to the success or failure of an implementation, and how to create and follow through successfully on an implementation project. By following the recommendations made, not only those regarding how to implement, but also those regarding what not to do, a manager will have a much higher chance of success. With this information in hand, the reader can now confidently peruse the remaining chapters, which are full of payroll best practices. The reader will be able to select those practices having the best chance of a successful implementation based on his or her specific circumstances, such as the funding and time available, as well as any obstacles, such as entrenched employees or corporate intransigence pertaining to new projects.

2

Employee Time Tracking

This chapter addresses those 11 best practices having a direct impact on the efficiency and effectiveness of employee time tracking. As noted in Exhibit 2.1, there are six relatively simple ways to reduce the amount of information collected as part of the timekeeping process as well as reduce the number of people who are required to track their time. The remaining five best practices all involve the use of technology to improve the accuracy of timekeeping (bar-coded time clocks), collect information more easily (time tracking with mobile phones or Web-based time tracking), improve control over the process (biometric time clocks), or ensure that employees update their time records more speedily (automated reminders).

Exhibit 2.1   Employee Time Tracking Best Practices Summary

	Best Practice	Cost	Install Time
2.1	Switch to salaried positions	💵	⏰ ⏰
2.2	Reduce the number of pay codes	💵	⏰
2.3	Eliminate personal leave days	💵	⏰
2.4	Use honor system to track vacation and sick time	💵	⏰
2.5	Avoid job costing through the payroll system	💵	⏰
2.6	Use exception time reporting	💵 💵	⏰ ⏰
2.7	Use bar-coded time clocks	💵 💵	⏰ ⏰
2.8	Use biometric time clocks	💵 💵	⏰ ⏰
2.9	Install a Web-based timekeeping system	💵 💵	⏰ ⏰ ⏰
2.10	Install automated timesheet reminders	💵 💵	⏰ ⏰
2.11	Track time with mobile phones	💵 💵	⏰ ⏰

Of the best practices noted in this chapter, reducing the number of pay codes, avoiding job cost tracking, and exception time recording are highly recommended on the grounds that timekeeping simplification vastly reduces the payroll department's job and improves the accuracy of what little information is still required. Of the automated timekeeping systems noted here, bar-coded time clocks have proven their effectiveness over many years, and Web-based systems are extremely useful for tracking the time of employees located in widely distributed locations.

2.1 Switch to Salaried Positions

When processing payroll, it is evident that the labor required to process the payroll for a salaried person is significantly lower than for an hourly employee; there is no change in the payroll data from period to period for a salaried person, whereas the number of hours worked must be recomputed for an hourly employee every time the payroll is processed. Therefore, it is reasonable to shift as many employees as possible over to salaried positions from hourly ones in order to reduce the labor of calculating payroll.

Implementing this best practice can be a significant problem; it is not under the control of the payroll department, as it is up to the managers of other departments to switch people over to salaried positions, so the payroll manager must persuade others to make the concept a reality. Another problem is that unions generally oppose this best practice, as they prefer to give their members the option to earn extra overtime pay. Finally, government regulations prohibit the conversion of some positions to salaried status, with the main determining criterion being that a salaried person must act with minimal supervision.

Given the issues just noted, it may seem impossible to implement this best practice. However, it is quite possible in some industries. The main factor for success is that the industry have few hourly workers to begin with. For example, a company with many highly educated employees, or one that performs limited manufacturing, may already have so many salaried employees that converting over the few remaining hourly employees to salaried positions becomes a minor cleanup issue.

Cost: 🖋   *Installation time:* 🕐 🕐

2.2 Reduce the Number of Pay Codes

Companies sometimes require their employees to select from a wide array of pay codes when recording their time in a payroll system. From an administrative perspective, these codes can include training, jury duty, holidays, vacation, sick time, bereavement leave, and family leave. In the manufacturing area, the number of codes can be overwhelming, including codes for such activities as receiving, putaway, picking, cross docking, case breakdown, and cycle counting—and that is just the warehouse. Usually the payroll staff is called to monitor charges to these pay codes and make adjustments where necessary.

The trouble with having a broad range of pay codes is that the resulting data do not normally yield any improvement in company operations. Instead, once time is compiled initially within each pay code, the cost accountant usually finds that the proportions of time spent on each activity do not change very much over time. Thus, the extra labor required to charge time to them and correct a multitude of pay codes only affirms that activities are usually in a steady state and do not require much monitoring.

A better approach is to have as many employees as possible charge their time to a single pay code that needs to be altered only on an exception basis (see best practice 2.6, "Use Exception Time Reporting"). When the cost accounting staff needs additional information about specific activities, it can conduct a periodic review and collect the information itself, rather than requiring the payroll department to collect this information for it.

Cost: *Installation time:*

2.3 Eliminate Personal Leave Days

A common task for the payroll staff is to track the vacation time employees earn and use either manually or automatically. Depending on the level of automation, this task can require some portion of staff time every week on an ongoing basis. Some companies then take the additional step of accruing and tracking the usage of personal leave days, which are essentially the same thing as vacation time, but tracked under a different name. By having both vacation and personal leave days, the payroll staff must track data in both categories, which doubles the work required to simply track vacation time.

A reasonable, and easily implemented, best practice is to convert personal leave days into vacation days and eliminate the extra category of time off. By doing so, the payroll staff can cut in half the time it devotes to analyzing employee vacation time. The human resources (HR) department is the only department that may resist this change, as HR likes to offer a variety of benefits to match those offered by other companies; for example, if a competitor offers personal leave days, then so should the company. Although the problem is only a matter of semantics, it can cause difficulty with implementing the simpler system.

Cost: 💰   *Installation time:* ⏰

2.4 Use Honor System to Track Vacation and Sick Time

It is common for the payroll staff to be in charge of tracking the vacation and sick time used by employees. Doing this involves sending out forms for employees to fill out whenever they take time off, usually requiring their supervisor's signature. Upon receipt, the payroll staff logs the used time in the payroll system and files the forms away in employee personnel folders. If the payroll staff does not account for this information correctly in the payroll system, employees probably will spot the problem on their paycheck remittance advices the next time they are paid and will go to the payroll office to look into the matter—these inquiries take up staff time, as does the paperwork tracking effort.

When used with some control features, it is possible to completely eliminate the tracking of vacation and sick time by the payroll staff. Under this scenario, employees are placed on the honor system of tracking their own vacation and sick time. Although this system keeps the payroll staff from having to track this information, there is also a strong possibility that some employees will abuse the situation and take extra time. There are two ways to avoid this problem. One is to institute a company-wide policy that automatically wipes out all earned vacation and sick time at the end of each calendar year, which has the advantage of limiting the amount of vacation and sick time to which an employee can claim that he or she is entitled. This step mitigates a company's losses if a dishonest employee leaves the company and claims payment for many hours of vacation and sick time that may go back for years. The other way to avoid the problem is to switch the tracking role to employee supervisors. These people are in the best position to see when employees are taking time off and can track that time much more easily than can the payroll staff. In short, with some relatively minor control changes, it is possible to use an honor system for the tracking of employee vacation and sick time.

Cost: *Installation time:*

2.5   Avoid Job Costing through the Payroll System

Some controllers have elaborate cost accounting systems set up that accumulate a variety of costs from many sources, to be used sometimes for activity-based costing and more frequently for job costing. One of these costs is labor, which sometimes is accumulated through the payroll system. When this is done, employees use lengthy time cards on which they record the time spent on many activities during the day, resulting in vastly longer payroll records than would otherwise be the case. This is a problem when the payroll staff is asked to sort through and add up all of the job-costing records, because it increases the workload of the payroll personnel by an order of magnitude. In addition, the payroll staff may be asked to enter the job-costing information that it has compiled into the job-costing database, which is yet another task that gets in the way of processing the payroll.

The obvious solution is to keep job costing separate from the payroll function, thereby vastly reducing the amount of work the payroll staff must complete as well as shrinking the number of opportunities for calculation errors. However, this step may meet with opposition from those people who need the job-costing records. There are several ways to avoid conflict over the issue. One is to analyze who is charging time to various projects or activities and see if the proportions to time charged vary significantly over time; if they do not, there is no reason to continue tracking job-costing information for hours worked. Another possibility is to split the functions so that the payroll staff collects its payroll data independently of the job-costing data collection, which can be handled by someone else. Either possibility will keep the job-costing function from interfering with the orderly collection of timekeeping information.

Cost: 💸　　　　*Installation time:* 🕐

2.6 Use Exception Time Reporting

Most employees work a standard 40-hour week and perform the same tasks over and over again, week after week. However, the typical time-tracking system requires them to complete a time sheet every week. Because they see no point in submitting the same information every week, employees continually forget to submit time sheets on a timely basis, which means that the payroll staff has to spend time contacting them with reminders. Thus, everyone wastes a considerable amount of time to submit the same time-keeping information every week.

In situations where hours worked are essentially the same on an ongoing basis, a good alternative is to create a default time record in the timekeeping system and to require employees to change it only if they have non-standard hours to report, such as overtime or a short workweek. A lesser alternative for companies using a computer-based timekeeping system is to install a single button on-screen that employees can press if they simply want to copy forward their time sheet from the preceding week. Yet another variation applicable to salaried employees is for them to submit a time sheet only when they are recording paid time off, such as vacation, sick, jury duty, or military time.

This solution works less well when employees are charging their time to specific jobs that change frequently. If these are billable jobs for which time recording must be accurate, there is little opportunity to use this best practice. However, if charging to jobs is for internal cost accounting purposes and not required by an external entity, it is possible that the cost accounting staff can be convinced to reduce or eliminate their time-tracking requirements on the grounds that the labor component of most jobs in the production area is only a small component of the total cost and that the cost of time tracking is not worth the additional cost information.

Cost: 💸 💸　　　　*Installation time:* 🕐 🕐

2.7 Use Bar-Coded Time Clocks

The most labor-intensive task in the payroll area is calculating hours worked for hourly employees. To do so, a payroll clerk must collect all of the employee time cards for the most recently completed payroll period, manually accumulate the hours listed on the cards, and discuss missing or excessive hours with supervisors. This is a lengthy process with a high error rate, due to the large percentage of missing start or stop times on time cards. Employees usually find any errors as soon as they are paid, resulting in possibly confrontational visits to the payroll staff, demanding an immediate adjustment to their pay with a manual check. These changes disrupt the payroll department and introduce additional inefficiencies to the process.

The solution is to install a computerized time clock. This clock requires an employee to swipe a uniquely identified card through a reader on its side. The card is encoded with either a magnetic strip or a bar code that contains the employee's identification number. Once the swipe occurs, the clock automatically stores the date and time and downloads this information on request to the payroll department's computer, where special software automatically calculates the hours worked and also highlights any problems for additional research (i.e., missed card swipes). Many of these clocks can be installed throughout a large facility or at outlying locations so that employees can record their time conveniently, no matter where they may be. More advanced clocks also track the time periods when employees are supposed to arrive and leave and require a supervisor's password for card swipes outside of that time period; this feature allows for greater control over employee work hours. Many of these systems also issue absence reports, so that supervisors can tell who has not shown up for work. Thus, an automated time clock eliminates much low-end clerical work, while at the same time providing new management tools for supervisors.

Before one purchases such a clock, its limitations should be recognized. The most important one is cost. Such clocks cost $2,000 to $3,000 each, or they can be leased for several hundred dollars per month. If several clocks are needed, this can add up to a substantial investment. In addition, outlying time clocks that must download their information to a computer at a distant location require their own phone line, which represents an additional monthly payment to the phone company. There also may be a fee for using the software on the central computer that summarizes all the incoming payroll information. Given these costs, most commonly bar-coded time clocks are used only in those situations in which there are so many hourly employees that a significant savings in the payroll department results from their installation.

Also, employees will lose their swipe cards. To encourage them to keep their cards in a safe place, they can be charged a small fee for replacements.

Most hourly employees are used to paper-based time cards that have their start and stop times punched onto them. When a bar-coded time clock is installed, employees lose the security of seeing this record of their hours worked. Instead, they swipe a card through the clock and never see any evidence of time worked. To overcome the loss of security that comes from this changeover, the accounting staff should show the hourly personnel how the new clock works and where the data are stored, so that they can gain some assurance that their time data will not be lost. If there is an option that allows them to look up information on the time clock's LCD display, they should receive training in how to do this; in addition, a procedure could be posted next to the clock that shows how to obtain this information. It is also useful to install a set of green and red lights next to the scanner, with the green light flashing when a successful scan has been completed (and the red light indicating the reverse).

Cost: 💵 💵   *Installation time:* 🕐 🕐

2.8 Use Biometric Time Clocks

The bar-coded time clocks noted in the previous best practice represent an excellent improvement in the speed and accuracy with which employee time data can be collected. However, they suffer from an integrity flaw: Employees can use each other's badges to enter and exit from the payroll system. This means that some employees may be paid for hours when they were never really on-site at all.

A division of Ingersoll-Rand called Recognition Systems has surmounted this problem with the use of biometric time clocks (which can be seen at *www.handreader.com*). This reader requires an employee to place his or her hand on a sensor, which matches its size and shape to the dimensions already recorded for that person in a central database. The time entered into the terminal then will be recorded against the payroll file of the person whose hand was just measured. Thus, only employees who are on-site can have payroll hours credited to them. The company sells a variation on the same machine, called the HandKey, which is used to control access to secure areas. These systems have a secondary benefit, which is that no one needs an employee badge or pass key; these tend to be lost or damaged over time, and so represent a minor headache for the accounting or HR staffs, who must track them. In a biometric monitoring environment, all an employee needs is a hand.

These monitoring devices are expensive and require significant evidence of "buddy punching" to justify their cost. If these clocks are intended to replace bar-coded time clocks, then there is no projected labor savings from reducing the manual labor of the payroll personnel (because this advantage was already covered by the bar-coded clocks), leaving only the savings from buddy punching to justify their purchase.

The same lack of time-punched data exists in this case as was noted earlier for the bar-coded time clock. Again, it can be resolved by meeting with the hourly personnel to show them how their time data are collected, stored, and summarized and how to access this information on the time clock if the device has such data available.

Cost: 　　　　*Installation time:*

2.9　Install a Web-Based Timekeeping System

Although the use of bar-coded or biometric time clocks certainly solves a variety of timekeeping problems in environments where many employees are clustered together, the approach does not work well where employees are scattered over a wide area. It is not efficient for these employees to travel long distances to the time clocks to record their time, and the clocks are too expensive to multiply into every possible employee location. In these cases, the usual solution is to have employees fill out paper time sheets and fax them to the payroll department. Doing this requires employee access to a fax machine and also involves some risk that incoming time sheets will be lost at the fax machine. Further, the payroll staff may not punch the information on these time sheets into the payroll database for several days, which delays management access to the information. Finally, there is a risk that some information will be keypunched incorrectly.

A good solution is to set up a Web-based timekeeping system. Many employees now have Internet access and so can easily call up a screen that simulates a time card and enter their hours worked. In such a system, the payroll staff has no keypunching duties at all, the online system can warn employees of obvious keypunching errors on the spot, and timekeeping data are available much more quickly to management. This approach also gives employees more visibility into their own data, because they should be able to review previous time sheets, as well as verify their accrued and unused vacation and sick time balances through the online system.

Web-based timekeeping systems are becoming widely available through the larger payroll outsourcing suppliers. These products include ADP's ezLaborManager product, Cignify Corporation's PeopleNet product, and TALX Corporation's FastTime product. These products allow employees to charge time against a wide range of labor accounts. Using one of these outsourced solutions is particularly appealing if the payroll processing function is already outsourced, because the supplier can port the input data directly into its payroll application automatically, resulting in even less payroll processing work by the payroll department.

An alternative is to construct an in-house Web-based system, which may be more useful in companies that have closely integrated their timekeeping systems to a job billing system. Under this more customized approach, a logical configuration is to have employees enter time not only against a job number, but also to a labor code that translates into a specific billable hourly rate. The resulting reports should specify exactly who worked on a customer project during what time period, how many hours they worked, their billable rate, and the total charge being invoiced to the customer. Although this type of system requires considerable programming effort, the result is excellent automation not only of the timekeeping process, but of the billing process as well.

Cost: 💵 💵   *Installation time:* ⏱ ⏱ ⏱

2.10   Install Automated Time Sheet Reminders

The payroll staff may spend a considerable amount of time reminding employees to complete their time sheets, so they can be paid on time. This is an especially difficult problem when employees are traveling a great deal and are difficult to reach.

If a company uses a computer-based timekeeping system, the computer can determine automatically when time sheets have not been submitted and can automatically issue an e-mail notice to each laggard employee. It also can continue to do this on a repetitive basis, and issue a notice to an employee's supervisor if the time sheet has not been submitted within a certain number of notices.

This solution does not work well if some employees either do not have regular access to e-mail or do not use it, although it will still probably reduce the amount of follow-up contacts that the payroll staff must make. Also, this approach requires some custom programming work to achieve, as well as some tracking mechanism for determining who is a person's direct supervisor (if reminder e-mails are to be sent to supervisors as well).

Cost: 💵 💵   *Installation time:* 🕐 🕐

2.11   Track Time with Mobile Phones

When employees are occupied with off-site service jobs, such as copier repair, security monitoring, or landscaping work, it is difficult to track the exact amount of time they spend on each job. Instead, they tend to wait until they are back in the office and then jot down their billable time from memory. If they are paid based on their billable hours, this process introduces a great deal of uncertainty into the determination of their payroll hours. The use of a Web-based timekeeping system is not a good solution, because it requires Web access and a computer, which are not always available to this type of employee.

The solution is to incorporate a timekeeping system into a GPS-enabled cell phone. Under this approach, a company acquires a cell phone and associated Nextel service contract for each employee, and then signs up for the WorkTrack service of Aligo (accessible through *www.aligo.com*). For a monthly fee, this service allows employees to punch their job start and stop times directly into the phone, which transmits this information as a text message that the payroll staff can access through a simple Web browser. No other hardware or software is required; the text messages are sent to Aligo, which handles the reformatting of the resulting data for access through the Web. The system also allows the payroll staff to download standard time reports, as well as track employee locations on a map (which is useful for determining which people to send to another customer location). The system also can be used to push text messaging information back to users through the cell phones.

By using this approach, employees no longer have to complete time sheets manually, while the payroll staff can summarize payroll data more rapidly and the billing staff can issue invoices to customers within minutes of a job being completed in the field.

Cost: 💵 💵   *Installation time:* ⏰ ⏰

3

Employee Benefits
and Deductions

This chapter contains 15 best practices related to increased efficiencies for the handling of employee benefits and deductions. The first five items relate to reductions in workload, rather than taking any proactive action at all—for example, not allowing employees to pay for purchases through payroll deductions and avoiding the recognition of group term life insurance income by putting a hard cap on the maximum amount of insurance coverage allowed. Then a series of best practices cover the automation of various functions, including the tracking of vacations, options, and garnishments, as well as pension plan enrollment. Finally, there are a pair of major improvements related to giving employees a self-service capability over their benefits and deductions, thereby taking a considerable amount of data entry work completely away from the payroll staff.

A summary of the benefit and deduction best practices, including a ranking of their costs and installation time, is shown in Exhibit 3.1.

Of the best practices presented here, only four have any significant implementation cost: option tracking, vacation posting, and two types of self-service. Of these, the self-service improvements will have a major impact on departmental efficiency. Most of the other best practices can be implemented quickly, resulting in small but immediate improvements.

3.1 Prohibit Deductions for Employee Purchases

Many companies allow their employees to use corporate discounts to buy products through them. For example, a company may have obtained a large discount on furniture from a supplier. Its employees buy at the discounted rate and then have the deductions subtracted from their paychecks in

Exhibit 3.1   Employee Benefits and Deductions Best Practices Summary

	Best Practice	Cost	Install Time
3.1	Prohibit deductions for employee purchases	💵	🕐
3.2	Disallow prepayments	💵	🕐
3.3	Minimize payroll deductions	💵	🕐
3.4	Cap group term life insurance coverage at the IRS exclusion limit	💵	🕐
3.5	Charge employees a fee for garnishment processing	💵	🕐
3.6	Isolate in-pats and ex-pats in separate pay groups	💵	🕐
3.7	Include accrued vacation in the payroll remittance	💵	🕐
3.8	Post vacation information in the timekeeping system	💵 💵	🕐 🕐
3.9	Automate 401(k) plan enrollment	💵	🕐 🕐
3.10	Grant employees immediate 401(k) eligibility	💵	🕐 🕐
3.11	Automate garnishment transactions	💵	🕐
3.12	Automate option tracking	💵 💵 💵	🕐 🕐
3.13	Create employee self-service for payroll changes	💵 💵	🕐 🕐
3.14	Create employee self-service for benefit changes	💵 💵 💵	🕐 🕐 🕐
3.15	Link employees to the withholding calculator of the IRS	💵	🕐

convenient installments. Some employees make excessive use of this benefit, purchasing all kinds of supplies through the company; accordingly, often a small minority of employees makes the bulk of these purchases. The problem for the payroll staff is that it must keep track of the total amount that each employee owes the organization and gradually deduct the amount owed from successive paychecks. If an employee has multiple purchases, the payroll staff must recalculate the amount to be deducted constantly. Depending on the number of employees taking advantage of purchases through the company, this process can have a measurable impact on the efficiency of the payroll department.

The solution is to prohibit employee purchases through the organization. By doing so, all the extra paperwork associated with employee purchases is swept away immediately.

Although this best practice is a good one for most companies to implement, it should be cleared with senior management first. The reason is that some employees may be so accustomed to purchasing through the company that they will be rudely surprised by the change, which may be a condition that management wants to avoid (especially if the change will bother valuable employees). Also, some companies have valid reasons for allowing employee purchases, such as steel-toed boots or safety clothing that is necessary for performing their jobs.

As noted, this best practice should be reviewed with all key department managers and senior management before being made public. Also, any employees who currently are having deductions taken from their paychecks for past purchases should be grandfathered into the new rule, so that they are not forced to pay off the remaining amounts due suddenly.

Cost: *Installation time:*

3.2 Disallow Prepayments

Many employees do not have the monetary resources to see them through until the next payday. Their solution is to request a pay advance, which is deducted from their next paycheck. Complying with such requests is a humane gesture on the part of the payroll manager, but it plays havoc with the efficiency of the payroll department. Whenever such a request is made, the payroll staff must manually calculate the taxes to take out of the payment, then manually cut a check and have it signed. However, the inefficiencies are not yet over. In addition, the staff must manually enter the pay advance in the computer system so that the amount is properly deducted from the next paycheck. For larger advances, it may be necessary to make deductions over several paychecks, which requires even more work. Furthermore, if an employee quits work before earning back the amount of the advance, the company has just incurred a loss. Clearly, paycheck prepayments do not help the efficiency of the payroll department. This problem is particularly significant in organizations where the average pay level is near the minimum wage, because the recipients may not have enough money to meet their needs.

The best practice that solves this problem seems simple but can be difficult to implement. One must create a rule that no paycheck prepayments will be issued, which effectively ends the extra processing required of the payroll staff.

The trouble with this rule is that a needy employee usually can present such a good case for a pay advance that exceptions will be made; over time these exceptions grind away at the rule, until it is completely ignored. Other managers will assist in tearing down the rule by claiming that they will lose good employees if advances are not provided to them. The best way to support this rule is to form an association with a local lending institution that specializes in short-term loans. Then employees who request advances can be directed to the lending institution, which will arrange for an interest-bearing loan to them. When this arrangement exists, it is common for employees to tighten their budgets rather than pay the extra interest charged for use of the lender's money. This procedure improves employee finances while increasing the processing efficiency of the payroll staff.

One must be sure to arrange for alternative employee financing *before* setting up a no-advance rule, in order to be certain that alternative financing will be available to employees. Then it is wise to go over the rule with all employees several weeks before it is to be implemented, so that they will have fair warning of the change. Also, brochures available in the payroll department should describe the services of the lending institution, as well as contact information and directions for reaching it.

Cost: 💸   Installation time: 🕐

3.3 Minimize Payroll Deductions

A company can offer a large number of benefits to its employees, many of which require some sort of deduction from payroll. For example, a company can set up deductions for employee medical, dental, life, and supplemental life insurance, flexible spending account deductions for medical insurance or child care payments, as well as 401(k) deductions and 401(k) loan deductions. If there are many employees and many deduction types, the payroll staff can be snowed under at payroll processing time by the volume of changes that occur continually in this area. Also, whenever there is a change in the underlying cost of insurance provided to the company, the company commonly passes along some portion of these costs to the employees, resulting in a massive updating of deductions for all employees who take that particular type of insurance. These changes not only take time away from other, more value-added payroll tasks, but they also are subject to error, so that adjustments must be made later to correct the errors, which requires even more staff time.

There are several ways to address this problem. One is to eliminate the employee-paid portion of some types of insurance. For example, if the cost to the company for monthly dental insurance is $20 per employee and the related deduction is only $2 per person, management can elect to pay for the entire cost, rather than burden the payroll staff with the tracking of this trivial sum. Another alternative is to eliminate certain types of benefits, such as supplemental life insurance or 401(k) loans, in order to eliminate the related deductions. Yet another alternative is to create a policy that limits employee changes to any benefit plans, so employees can make only a small number of changes per year. This approach eliminates the continual changing of deduction amounts in favor of just a few large bursts of activity at prescheduled times during the year. A very good alternative is to create a benefit package for all employees that requires a single deduction of the same amount for everyone or for a group (i.e., one deduction for single employees and another for employees with families); employees can then pick and choose the exact amount of each type of benefit they want within the boundaries of each benefit package, without altering the amount of the underlying deduction. This last alternative has the unique advantage of consolidating all deductions into a single item, which is much simpler to administer. Any of these approaches to the problem will reduce the number or timing of deduction changes, thereby reducing the workload of the payroll staff.

Cost: *Installation time:*

3.4 Cap Group Term Life Insurance Coverage at the IRS Exclusion Limit

The IRS currently allows companies to exclude from their employees' reportable income the value of company-provided group term life insurance, up to a maximum of $50,000 of coverage. However, if a company provides coverage above this amount, it must be included in employee income, using an IRS premium table, and is subject to social security and Medicare taxes. The calculation of this income is relatively complex. The payroll department first must determine the subset of employees receiving insurance over $50,000, calculate the average amount of coverage for the calendar year (since there may have been a coverage change during the year), determine the amount of this average coverage exceeding $50,000, and then multiply the excess coverage by a cost rate determined by the IRS, which varies by employee age. This process can be automated, but is more commonly derived through an electronic spreadsheet calculation. Once the amount of income is determined, the payroll staff must record this amount as employee payroll at year-end, to appear in their W-2 forms.

Given the complexity of the benefit calculation, as well as the extra effort needed to record the resulting income information, there is some incentive not to pay life insurance exceeding the IRS exclusion limit. The simplest approach is to adopt a company policy whereby the maximum group term life insurance coverage automatically matches the IRS exclusion rate. This policy will be opposed by various factions within the company who want the benefit and do not care about extra work by the payroll staff; however, this approach may be more palatable if the coverage reduction is matched with an offsetting coverage increase in some other part of the employee benefits package.

Cost: 🪙   Installation time: ⏰

3.5 Charge Employees a Fee for Garnishment Processing

When an employee is garnished for any reason (i.e., tax liens or child support), the payroll department must take the time to set up an automatic deduction in the payroll system, as well as schedule ongoing payments to whatever court authorized the garnishment, which can involve a considerable amount of effort. Alternatively, if a company uses an outside garnishment service provided as part of a payroll outsourcing contract, it will be charged by the payroll supplier to set up and monitor the garnishment.

Many garnishment orders allow a company to charge a fee to the employee for each garnishment deduction, or else a maximum fee per month.

Whatever the charge may be, one should always take it. The effort required to do so is extremely small, and because it is the employee's fault that a garnishment is occurring at all, the company has every right to extract a fee in exchange for spending so much time on this work.

Cost: 💵   *Installation time:* ⏰

3.6 Isolate In-Pats and Ex-Pats in Separate Pay Groups

When a company has international locations, it is likely to have two sets of employees with special needs: in-pats (foreign citizens who work in the United States) and ex-pats (U.S. citizens who work in other countries). A nonresident in-pat (i.e., someone without a green card) may be subject to a variety of tax treaties and related payroll exceptions that can cause the payroll department a considerable amount of extra effort, from the perspective of both tax withholdings and income reporting. Further, an in-pat may be required to pay social security taxes in both the United States and his or her home country, which may require the recognition of a separate form of income to recognize the gross-up income the company pays the in-pat employee to compensate for the loss caused by the social security deduction. Ex-pats are subject to a variety of additional types of income, such as danger pay, a cost-of-living allowance, a housing allowance, and tax equalization (to guarantee that they are subject only to the same tax rate they would have experienced if they were still living in the United States); all of these forms of income must be recognized within the payroll system. Also, the payroll department needs to know where on the annual W-4 form it is supposed to itemize these payments to ex-pats. Clearly, the treatment of in-pats and ex-pats is a considerable headache for the payroll department.

Although there is no easy way to deal with the special payroll requirements of these employees, it is at least possible to isolate them in a separate set of pay groups in the payroll system, so similar employees requiring similar payment and withholding treatments can be clustered together. This treatment allows the payroll staff to process their payroll transactions more efficiently as a group, rather than trying to pick them out from the mass of regular employees in the payroll system.

Cost: 💵   *Installation time:* ⏰

3.7 Include Accrued Vacation in the Payroll Remittance

The accounting topic that is of the most interest to the most employees is how much accrued vacation time they have left. In most companies, this information is calculated manually by the payroll staff, so employees troop down to the payroll department once a month (and more frequently during the prime summer vacation months) to see how much vacation time they have left to use. Employees constantly coming in to find out this information is a major interruption to the payroll staff, because it happens at all times of the day, never allowing them to settle down into a comfortable work routine. If many employees request this information, it can result in a considerable loss of efficiency for the payroll staff.

A simple way to keep employees from bothering the payroll staff is to include the vacation accrual in employee paychecks. The information appears on the payroll remittance, showing the annual amount of accrued vacation, net of any used time. Employees who receive this information in every paycheck have no need to inquire in the payroll office, eliminating a major hindrance.

There are several points to consider before implementing this best practice. First, the payroll system must be equipped with a vacation accrual option. If not, the software must be customized to allow for the calculation and presentation of this information, which may cost more to implement than the projected efficiency savings. Another problem is that the accrual system must be set up properly for each employee when it is originally installed, or else outraged employees will crowd into the payroll office, causing more disruption than was the case before. This start-up problem is caused by employees with different numbers of allowed vacation days per year, as well as some with unused vacation time from the previous year that must be carried forward into the next year. If this information is not reflected accurately in the automated vacation accrual system when it is implemented, employees will hasten to the payroll department to have this information corrected at once. Another problem is that the accruals must be adjusted over time to reflect changes. Otherwise, once again, employees will interrupt the staff to notify them of changes, thereby offsetting the value of the entire system. For example, employees may switch from two to three weeks of allowed vacation at the fifth anniversary of their hiring. The payroll department must have a schedule of when each person's vacation accrual amount changes to the three-week level, or the employee will come in and complain. If these problems can be overcome, using vacation accruals becomes a relatively simple means of improving the efficiency of the payroll department.

It helps to have a few simple procedures in place to make this best practice function more efficiently. For example, one should have a schedule available in the payroll department that itemizes the dates on which employees with sufficient seniority are scheduled to have increases in their allowed vacation amounts; a review of this document should be included in the monthly departmental schedule of activities, so that accrual changes can be made in a timely manner. Also, the payroll staff should be trained in the proper data entry into the payroll system for any vacation hours taken by employees. Finally, one should create a procedure for making changes to the data in the automated vacation accrual system, so that the staff can correct errors in the system.

Cost: 💰   *Installation time:* 🕰

3.8 Post Vacation Information in the Timekeeping System

The preceding best practice recommended adding vacation information to the payroll remittance. However, that approach requires a payroll staff person to manually enter payroll information from a separate vacation tracking system into the payroll system. Also, it does not prevent employees from going to the payroll department to ask theoretical vacation questions, such as how much vacation time they will have accrued by some future date (i.e., year-end or the date when their scheduled vacation begins).

The best way to eliminate all vacation-related problems is to create a vacation tracking application that is directly tied to the company timekeeping system and available to employees via the company intranet. By doing so, there is a direct linkage between hours entered by employees and the vacation calculation, which allows them to model earned vacation time based on any date they choose to enter, based on the hours worked and vacation hours previously taken that they have entered into the system.

This approach requires custom programming. The design should include a table listing standard vacation amounts for varying levels of seniority (i.e., three weeks of vacation after five years of service, four weeks after ten years, etc.), as well as a mechanism for carrying forward maximum amounts of vacation time into the following year and some provision for overrides to the system with supervisory approval. This programming work can prove complex.

Cost: 💸 💸   *Installation time:* 🕰 🕰

3.9 Automate 401(k) Plan Enrollment

In smaller organizations, the payroll department is tasked with the management of 401(k) plan additions, changes, and deletions. This is not an efficient process, for someone must arrange for a meeting with all employees who have now been working for the minimum amount of time, as specified in the plan documentation, explain the plan's features to them, wait for them to take the plan materials home for review, and, finally, enter the returned documents into the system of the 401(k) provider. The process is a lengthy and time-consuming one.

An alternative is to enroll employees in the 401(k) plan automatically, a process known as a negative election, because employees must make a decision not to be enrolled in the plan, rather than the reverse. This approach has the considerable advantage of reducing the paperwork needed to enter a person into the 401(k) plan, because it is done as part of the hiring process, along with all other paperwork needed to set up a new employee.

There are only minor downsides to this best practice. With more employees in the plan, the 401(k) service provider will charge somewhat higher fees (typically they are charged on a per-person basis). Also, there will still be some paperwork associated with those employees who *do* make a negative election. Finally, employees who are added to the 401(k) plan through this method and who might otherwise not have chosen to be in the plan tend to be at the lower end of the income stratum, so it is more likely that they will want to take out loans against their invested funds, which calls for more paperwork.

Cost: 💸   *Installation time:* 🕰 🕰

3.10 Grant Employees Immediate 401(k) Eligibility

The most common way to enroll employees into a company's 401(k) pension plan is to make them wait either 90 days or a year from the date of hire. This process calls for the maintenance of a list of dates for newly hired employees that must be watched to ascertain when people become available for this benefit. Then they must be contacted and scheduled for a short lecture about how the plan works and how to invest in it. Then they complete paperwork to enroll, which is forwarded to the payroll department so that deductions can be made from their paychecks for advancement to the 401(k) plan administrator. All of the steps can be compressed into the hiring process, as noted in best practice 3.9, "Automate 401(k) Plan Enrollment." However, the issue can be taken one step further by not only completing all of the paperwork at the time of hire, but also by allowing *immediate* participation in the plan at the time of hire. This method represents less a matter of improved efficiency than of giving new employees a fine new benefit, for they can begin investing at once, which may lead to a reduced level of employee turnover.

The main problem with this best practice is that employee turnover tends to be fairly high during the first few months of work, since employees are in an evaluation period and are more likely to be terminated. Additional paperwork for the payroll staff to handle withheld funds on behalf of the now-departed employees can result.

Cost: 🖎 *Installation time:* 🕰🕰

3.11 Automate Garnishment Transactions

When the payroll department receives a garnishment order, it must calculate an employee's disposable income, determine the appropriate deductible amount in light of any other garnishment orders applicable to the same employee, enter deduction codes in the payroll system, pay the garnishing entity, and monitor when the garnishment will be completed. The workload can be substantial if there are a number of employees subject to garnishment orders. Also, because remittances to garnishing entities are handled by a different group within the accounting department (accounts payable), it is possible that some payment instructions will be lost in transition, resulting in missing payments that can lay the company open to fines and penalties.

An excellent alternative is to enroll in a third-party wage garnishment processing service. This service is offered by some payroll outsourcing companies, such as ADP and Paychex. Under this arrangement, the payroll department sends garnishment information to the garnishment processing service, which continually tracks the correct deduction amount, monitors garnishment status, prioritizes garnishment orders, and makes payments to the garnishing entities. Because payroll outsourcing companies track state requirements for garnishments in considerable detail, they also tend to make more accurate garnishment payments. There is a fee for this service, which makes it cost effective only for larger companies.

The primary downside to this best practice is that it can be used only if a company already outsources its payroll calculations, because the supplier needs access to employee payroll information to calculate garnishment amounts and also sets up the garnishment deductions from the payroll.

Cost: 💸   *Installation time:* 🕰

3.12 Automate Option Tracking

When a large number of employees have company options, either the payroll or the human resources department will be the target of ongoing questions about the vesting, valuation, and tax implications of these options. Because the tax laws are so complex in this area, employees keep asking follow-up clarification questions, as well as requests to run what-if scenarios on what they should do under various circumstances. Given a large number of employees with many option grants, a major drain on company resources can result. In addition, a company runs the risk of giving bad advice to its employees, which may have legal repercussions if employees using this advice lose money through the exercise of options.

A solution for larger companies is to purchase an options tracking package, which they can use alternatively as an in-house solution or as a featured service on the external site of an application service provider. An example of such software is Express Options, which is sold by Transcentive, Inc. The system stores all options information in a single database, allowing one to handle multiple grant types, determine vesting schedules, track option exercises and cancellations, and provide employees with tax-related information. It also calculates option valuations, exports data to the company stock transfer agent, and provides a variety of reports for regulatory purposes. By using Transcentive's add-on product, Express Desktop, employees can access such information about their options as portfolio valuations based on different stock pricing assumptions, what-if modeling, transaction histories, and frequently asked questions. They also can place orders to exercise their options through the system.

For this type of service, one can expect to pay a minimum of $15,000 annually, with the price exceeding $300,000 per year for larger installations. Given its cost, this best practice is most applicable to corporations with at least several hundred option holders.

Cost: 💵 💵 💵   Installation time: 🕐 🕐

3.13 Create Employee Self-Service for Payroll Changes

Employees always want to make some sort of data change in the payroll system, such as changes to their direct deposit, withholding, address, name, and marital status information. The payroll staff must make all of these changes, as well as the inevitable corrections caused by errors in data entry. For example, when an employee first wants to set up direct deposit, she forwards this information to the payroll staff, who inputs it into whatever payroll software is in use. If the employee forwards incorrect information or if it is incorrectly keypunched into the system, it is rejected and must be dealt with again during the next payroll cycle. In addition, employees may switch bank accounts or want to split deposits into multiple accounts—all of which require additional work by the payroll staff. Depending on the number of employees, these types of changes can represent a significant ongoing effort.

The latest advance in the area of self-service is for payroll outsourcing companies to manage self-service Web sites on behalf of their clients, who merely provide a link to these sites from their intranet sites. ADP provides this service, and estimates that a customized site can be operational in as little as 30 days. The ADP site allows the payroll manager to upload a variety of employee-centric documents, such as the employee manual, company phone directory, payroll forms, and news releases. In addition to these basic functions, the site also allows employees to access their pay statements and W-2 forms, view their earnings history, check their remaining vacation time, see performance reviews, view their 401(k) plan balances, and verify their benefits elections. Other companies claiming to have self-service options available include Ceridian, DPSI, Geac, Hewitt Associates, Humanic Solutions, Kronos, and PayMaxx. However, the range of services offered varies considerably, as does the implementation time period.

An alternative is to construct this type of portal for an in-house legacy payroll system, but the programming effort required is so substantial that a company must have a considerable number of employees to make it worthwhile. Another alternative would be to install a self-service module if a company uses commercial off-the-shelf payroll software that already provides this functionality.

For example, employees can alter the bank routing and account numbers used for the direct deposit of their pay into bank accounts or change the amounts split between deposits to their savings and checking accounts. They also could use this approach to process requests for additional W-2 forms or to download files containing the employee manual or other relevant personnel information. Further, they can register for company training classes, update emergency contact information, and make time-off requests.

One of the more iterative processes in the payroll department is the handling of direct deposit information for employees.

Cost: 🪙 🪙   *Installation time:* 🕐 🕐

3.14 Create Employee Self-Service for Benefit Changes

A major task for the payroll staff is to meet with employees to go over the effect of any deduction changes they wish to make, calculate the changes, and enter them into the payroll database. This task can be particularly time-consuming if the number of possible deduction options is large, if employees are allowed to make deduction changes at any time, or if employees are not well educated regarding the impact of deduction changes on their net pay.

A particularly elegant best practice that resolves this problem is to give employees direct access to the deduction data so they can determine the impact of deduction changes themselves and enter the changes directly into the payroll database. To do so, one must construct an interface to the payroll database that lists all deductions taken from employee paychecks (with the exception of garnishments, which are set by law). However, this is not enough, for most deductions usually are tied to a benefit of some sort. For example, a deduction for a medical plan can be changed only if the underlying medical plan option is altered. Accordingly, an employee needs access to a split screen of information, with one side showing benefit options and the other side showing the employee's gross pay, all deductions, and net pay. This view allows one to modify deductions and watch the impact on net pay. Examples of deductions for which this data view will work are federal and state tax deductions, medical and dental plan coverage, life and disability insurance coverage, and pension plan deductions.

An example of this approach is the dental plan. On one side of the computer screen, an employee is presented with five dental plan options, all with different costs. The employee can scroll through the list and select any option, while watching the selection automatically change the payroll calculation on the other side of the screen. Once the employee finds the selection that works best, he or she presses a button to enter the change into the payroll system. Such a system should include some selection blocks so that employees cannot change deductions constantly; for example, the software may limit employees to one health plan change per year.

This approach completely eliminates all work by the payroll staff to enter deduction changes into the computer. An added benefit is that employees are responsible for their own data-entry mistakes. If they make an incorrect entry, they can go into the system themselves to correct it. In addition, the deduction modeling system just noted allows employees to determine precisely what their net pay will be, eliminating any surprises. In a more traditional system, employees might make a deduction change without realizing the full impact of the change on their net pay and end up back in the payroll office, demanding a reversion back to the old deduction level. Using the modeling system can eliminate such multiple visits from employees to payroll staff.

This system will work only if one is willing to invest a significant amount of software development effort to design an employee interface, as well as to provide either individual computers or central kiosks to employees so that they can use the system. Given its high cost, this system usually is found only in larger organizations with many employees, where the cost-benefit trade-off is obvious.

The software development effort required for this best practice is substantial, so it must be budgeted well in advance and gain the approval of whatever committee schedules the order in which development projects will be completed. Also, all benefit plan rules related to changes in the plans must be documented carefully, so that employees are not caught unawares; for example, many dental insurance plans cover the costs of major dental surgery only if participants have been in the plan for at least one year—the computer system must warn employees of this requirement before they switch to a different plan.

Cost: 💵 💵 💵   *Installation time:* ⏲ ⏲

3.15 Link Employees to the Withholding Calculator of the IRS

Even when notified to review their tax withholding amounts each year, employees tend to leave them alone and change them only at the last moment when they suddenly realize that the current withholding levels are either much too high or low. This causes problems for the payroll staff, who must deal with withholding changes on a rush basis, typically near employee tax filing time.

A good way to avoid the panic of withholding changes is to encourage employees to go to the online withholding calculator of the IRS. This tool walks employees through several screens, where they input a variety of information about their marital status, types of income, and various deduction levels before arriving at an estimated total tax liability, which it also conveniently converts into a specific number of allowances and additional withholdings (if any) to enter on their W-4 forms.

Unfortunately, the IRS keeps changing the Web address for this calculator, so it is best to access it through a Web search engine such as Google. One should enter the words "IRS Withholding Calculator" in the search engine to locate the IRS site. It may be useful to keep this link on the company intranet site, so employees can review their withholdings at any time.

Cost: 💵   *Installation time:* ⏲

4

Payroll Forms
and Reports

This chapter presents eight best practices related to payroll forms and reports, sorted in declining order of importance. First in priority is a general review of reports to see which ones can be eliminated permanently, followed by the posting of forms to the company intranet site for general access by employees. These two best practices yield the greatest improvement in departmental efficiency of all the items noted here. The next two items cover the issuance of information to employees in electronic format, while the subsequent best practice uses a standard pay raise report to force improvements in the speed of the raise-granting process. We then conclude with two electronic storage practices and a fax-back approach to issuing forms that is useful for employees having no computer access. A summary of the forms and reports, including a ranking of their costs and installation time, is shown in Exhibit 4.1.

Exhibit 4.1	Payroll Forms and Reports Best Practices Summary		
	Best Practice	**Cost**	**Install Time**
4.1	Eliminate reports	💵	🕐🕐
4.2	Post forms on an intranet site	💵	🕐🕐
4.3	Automate the annual W-4 review notice to employees	💵	🕐
4.4	Issue electronic W-2 forms to employees	💵	🕐🕐
4.5	Base pay raises on an automated step increase report	💵	🕐
4.6	Store W-2 forms on compact disc	💵	🕐
4.7	Store I-9 forms in an electronic format	💵💵	🕐🕐
4.8	Automate fax-back of payroll forms	💵💵💵	🕐🕐🕐

The best practices noted here are generally inexpensive and relatively easy to install, with the exception of the automated fax-back of payroll forms. However, several of the items require that a company outsource some portion of its payroll processing or send data to a third party for additional processing, because suppliers with specialized skills offer these functions; best practices falling into this category include electronic W-2 forms, W-2 storage, and I-9 storage.

4.1 Eliminate Reports

Most payroll departments are awash in reports. Typically, someone asks the department to generate a report, which it does—and continues to do for the foreseeable future because no one has told it to stop. The majority of these reports are really needed only once. Even though their use is limited, the department continues to churn them out because the recipients are not aware of the cost of creating them. A further problem is report distribution. It is common for someone who does not realize a report's expense to have it sent to everyone in the organization who might use it and to many who most certainly do not. Over time, the accumulation of all these reports and their associated distribution lists creates a startlingly large filing burden. Not only are these reports stored, in case someone needs them, but they are distributed, and it is the job of the payroll staff to do both things.

The obvious solution is to reduce the number of reports and the number of recipients. A common approach is simply to stop distributing reports and see who complains. However, this is not a very astute political move by the payroll manager; an abrupt halt to reporting can irritate the heads of any departments who are receiving the information. Instead, it is better to use these five steps:

1. *Issue a list of outstanding reports and distributions.* Sometimes it is sufficient to bring to the attention of other departments the extent of the report list that is being used. If issued along with a list of report recipients, as well as a plea from the payroll manager to review the lists and cross out any reports and recipients that are no longer needed, it is usually possible to put a considerable dent in the payroll department's reporting and filing chore.

2. *Notify recipients of the cost of reports.* If a simple notification of the number of reports does not result in any significant change, it may be

necessary to notify management of the total cost of creating and issuing these reports. If the cost is considerable, the management team may authorize the elimination of several additional reports.

3. *Combine reports.* Once the report list has been pruned with the previous steps, it is time to interview the report recipients and see what information on each report actually is being used. Then it may be possible to combine the data on several reports, resulting in fewer ones that are really needed.

4. *Charge recipients for reports.* If there are still a number of reports left to produce, it may be necessary to charge recipients for the cost of both creating and distributing the reports. Incurring an expense for information almost invariably causes department managers to take a serious look at cutting back on their use of reports.

5. *Post reports on the computer network.* This last option allows the payroll staff to avoid all distribution work by posting electronic reports on the computer network, where users can access it for themselves. This approach may not work for some reports that do not convert readily to a computer-readable format, nor is it available to those report recipients who do not have a computer or access to one.

Cost: 💸   *Installation time:* 🕐 🕐

4.2 Post Forms on an Intranet Site

Employees frequently come to the accounting department to ask for any of the variety of forms required for changes to their payroll status, such as the W-4 form of the IRS, address changes, flexible spending account sign-up or change forms, and so on. These constant interruptions interfere with the orderly flow of payroll work, especially when the department runs out of a form and must scramble to replenish its supplies.

This problem is neatly solved by converting all forms to Adobe Acrobat's PDF format and posting them on a company intranet site for downloading by all employees. By using this approach, no one ever has to approach the payroll staff for the latest copy of a form. Also, employees can download the required form from anywhere, rather than having to wait until they are near the payroll location to physically pick one up. Further, the payroll staff can update the PDF forms regularly on the intranet site, so there is no risk of someone using an old and outmoded form.

Converting a regular form to PDF format is simple. First, one purchases the Acrobat software from Adobe's Web site and installs it. Then one accesses a form in whatever software package it was originally constructed and prints it to "PDF Acrobat," which will now appear on the list of printers. There are no other steps—the PDF format is complete. The IRS also uses the PDF format for its forms, which can be downloaded from the *www.irs.gov* site and posted to the company intranet site.

Cost: 💸   *Installation time:* 🕐 🕐

4.3 Automate the Annual W-4 Review Notice to Employees

Under IRS regulations, every company is required to remind its employees to review their tax status as listed on their last signed W-4 forms (i.e., single/married status and number of tax withholdings), so they can file a new one if necessary. This reminder must be issued to employees no later than December 1 of each year. The payroll department can spend extra time issuing a formal reminder memo to all employees and spend even more time ensuring everyone receives it. The usual approach is to mail it to their homes, which requires folding, stuffing, and mailing the notice.

A simpler approach is to print a reminder notice on the paycheck remittance advice. Doing this can be arranged easily through the in-house payroll software or through the payroll supplier (if the function is outsourced). By doing so, the company incurs no extra distribution costs, because it already is distributing the remittance advices to employees.

Cost: 💸   *Installation time:* 🕐

4.4 Issue Electronic W-2 Forms to Employees

A large company can experience some difficulty in issuing W-2 forms to its employees if they are distributed over a wide area. The mailing cost of this distribution also can be expensive, especially if the employer wants proof of receipt, which calls for the use of more expensive overnight delivery services. This problem can be avoided by issuing electronic W-2 forms to employees, thereby avoiding all related postage costs.

The IRS has issued four specific regulations for the use of electronic W-2 forms:

1. Employees must give their consent to the receipt of an electronic W-2 form, and do so electronically, thereby showing proof that they are capable of receiving the electronic format in which the W-2 form will be sent.
2. The W-2 forms must contain all standard information that normally would be found on a paper W-2 form.
3. Employees must be notified that the forms have been posted on a Web site for their access and must receive instructions on how to access the information.
4. The access must be maintained through October 15 of the year following the calendar year to which it relates.

These regulations are not difficult to meet, and the use of a central Web site for storage of the information also allows the employer to determine precisely which W-2 forms have been accessed. However, it is likely that some employees who have minimal access to computers or who are not computer literate will not access their W-2 forms in this manner, requiring a last-minute distribution of W-2 forms to anyone who has not accessed their electronic copies. Also, paper-based W-2 forms still must be issued to any employees who left the company prior to the end of the calendar year. Thus, this best practice likely will result in only a partial electronic distribution of W-2 forms.

Electronic W-2 distribution is now available through several suppliers. An example is JAT Computer Consulting (*www.jatnet.com*). This company requires a data feed for W-2 information from its client companies and then posts the W-2 information on its Web site for access by company employees in PDF format. If errors are found in someone's W-2, it is also possible for a manager to access the site, alter the underlying information, and issue a revised W-2c form, which can be e-mailed to the employee or posted to the Web site for access at the employee's convenience. The site even provides an online employee consent form to have W-2 forms provided in an electronic format; JAT summarizes this approval information and sends it back to the company, which uses it to determine which employees still require a paper W-2 form. For these services, the company charges a database load fee that is volume-based, as well as a $0.40 usage fee per online transaction. There is also an archiving fee for W-2 information stored for prior years. Other suppliers offering a similar service include Skylight Financial (*www.skylight.net*) and TALX Corporation (*www.talx.com*).

Cost: 💵   *Installation time:* ⏱⏱

4.5 Base Pay Raises on an Automated Step Increase Report

One of the larger inefficiencies in the payroll department is the timely receipt and processing of pay raises. In many cases, managers are dilatory in forwarding approved pay raises, sometimes doing so months after they were supposed to have been processed. The result is rush processing of the raise in order to mitigate the ire of the affected employee, as well as the calculation of back pay in case the pay raise date is set to match the employee's one-year anniversary since his or her last raise date.

The situation can be improved by incorporating estimated pay raises into the annual budget and combining this information with scheduled employee raise anniversary dates. The result is a report listing the date on which each employee should receive a raise and the amount of that raise. The payroll manager can send this information to the department managers well in advance of the expected raise activation dates, so they will have proper notice of the upcoming event and can send back approvals or adjustments to the proposed raise amounts.

An extended use of this report is to employ it as the primary basis for pay raise documentation. The payroll manager sends the report to the department managers, with a request that the raises will go into effect at the amounts and on the dates indicated in the report, unless they notify the payroll manager otherwise. This is an excellent way to ensure that raises go into effect in a timely manner and is especially effective where some managers would otherwise be so slow in processing raise-related paperwork that employees would have to wait months for their raises.

Cost: 💵   *Installation time:* ⏱

4.6 Store W-2 Forms on Compact Disc

There always seem to be a few employees who claim that they have lost their W-2 forms or never received them in the mail, and need a replacement copy *right now*, so they can complete their tax returns. When these calls arrive, a payroll clerk must spend time rooting through the archives for the correct W-2 form and then make a copy for the employee. Doing this can easily represent 15 minutes of research time for each request—and there may be many such requests.

A good alternative for those companies subscribing to an outside payroll processing service is to have the service store all W-2 forms on a compact disc, which can then be searched using a variety of indexes to find the correct W-2 form quickly. Because this service is inexpensive, it is a cost-effective approach for all but the smallest companies. The service is provided by both ADP and Ceridian. A number of regional document imaging companies are capable of scanning W-2 forms into digital format for storage on compact disc, although this is a more expensive service and applicable only to companies that produce their own W-2 forms.

The main downside is that the compact disc contains private payroll information for the entire company and so should be stored in a secure location at all times.

Cost: ✎   *Installation time:* 🕐

4.7 Store I-9 Forms in an Electronic Format

Companies are required by law to have all employees provide proof of employment eligibility and verification. This information is documented on the Form I-9, which must be stored by the employer, usually in either the human resources or payroll department. Although not a large paperwork burden, the form represents yet another document that must be retained and that can be audited by the government.

A bill was passed by Congress late in 2004 that allows companies to retain electronic versions of I-9 forms. If a company were to take this approach, it could scan existing I-9 forms into a document management database, making it very easy to pull up document images in the event of an audit. Further, the bill allows the use of electronic signatures on I-9 forms, so all future form completions can be handled in electronic format, with no additional scanning of paper documents required. Even better, one could easily match the names on the document database to the current employee list to ensure that I-9 forms are on hand for all employees, resulting in an excellent control over the I-9 documentation process.

The main downside to this approach is the need to scan existing I-9 forms into a document management database, which may require the services of an outside scanning service.

Cost: 🪙 🪙   *Installation time:* ⏰ ⏰

4.8 Automate Fax-Back of Payroll Forms

A payroll clerk is the unofficial keeper of the payroll and human resources forms. Employees come to this person to collect these forms, which can vary from a request to change a payroll deduction to a request to change a pension deduction amount. If a company has many employees, or if it has many locations (which necessitates mailing forms to recipients), the chore of handing out forms can take up a large amount of staff time.

To avoid distributing forms to employees, an automated fax-back system can be set up. This best practice requires employees to contact a computer, either using a touch-tone phone or through the computer system, and request that the appropriate form be sent to a fax number close to the employee. Employees with computer access can download the forms directly, and either fill them out on their computers or print them, fill them out, and mail them back.

The computer has all of the forms digitized and stored in its memory, and can make the transmission with no human intervention. For example, an employee accesses the system through a computer, scrolls through a list of available forms, highlights the needed item, enters the send-to fax number, and logs off. The form arrives a few moments later.

Under a manual distribution system, it is common practice to issue large quantities of forms to outlying locations, so that the payroll staff does not constantly have to send small numbers of additional forms; however, these forms end up being used for a long time, frequently past the date when they become obsolete. An automated fax-back system eliminates this problem by having only the most recent version available for transmission. This is a boon to the payroll staff, who might otherwise receive old forms that do not contain key information, requiring them to contact employees to gather the missing data or even forcing employees to resubmit their requests on the latest forms.

In addition, the system can automatically send along an extra instruction sheet with each distributed form so that employees can easily fill out forms without having to call the payroll staff for assistance.

An automated fax-back system can be expensive, so all costs should be determined before beginning an implementation. The system includes a separate file server linked to one or more phone lines (for receiving touch-tone phone requests as well as for sending forms out to recipient fax machines), plus a scanner for digitizing payroll forms. The best way to justify these added costs is if there are a large number of employees to be serviced, which saves a large amount of staff time. Without enough employees to create a valid justification, the system should not be installed.

One must be sure to leave enough time in the implementation schedule to review the variety of fax-back systems on the market prior to making a purchase, as well as to configure the system and test it with employees. If the system has an option for document requests both by phone and computer, one should implement one at a time to ensure that each variation is properly set up.

Cost: 💵 💵 💵   *Installation time:* 🕐 🕐 🕐

5

Payments to Employees

This chapter contains 14 best practices, all related to the payment of employees. The chief focus of this set of recommendations is to switch both the issuance of payments and the delivery of related remittance advices (pay stubs) to an electronic format. Several recommendations are designed to force employees to use electronic payments, and two miscellaneous best practices bring up the end of the chapter.

The distribution of employee pay is one of the chief causes of payroll department inefficiency, so several of the recommendations noted in this chapter are crucial. First, one should make sure that all employees are paid electronically, either through direct deposit or pay cards. Next, one should convert to the electronic delivery of their remittance advices. By taking these two steps, the payroll department is in an excellent position to completely automate the pay distribution function. Direct deposit has been available for years, while pay cards are just now becoming widely available. Several payroll suppliers offer electronic access to remittance advices, so this last requirement is now becoming a cost-effective best practice too. Because it is less costly to implement all three of these functions when the payroll processing function is outsourced to a supplier offering the full range of these services, there may be an increasing trend in favor of more payroll outsourcing.

5.1 Use Direct Deposit

A major task for the payroll staff is to issue paychecks to employees. This task can be subdivided into five steps.

	Exhibit 5.1 Payments to Employees Best Practices Summary		
	Best Practice	**Cost**	**Install Time**
5.1	Use direct deposit	💵	⏰ ⏰
5.2	Stop delivering checks to employees at the office	💵	⏰
5.3	Pay employees through payroll cards	💵	⏰ ⏰
5.4	Offer clear cards to employees	💵	⏰ ⏰
5.5	Offer prepaid flexible spending account cards	💵	⏰ ⏰
5.6	Offer prepaid incentive cards	💵	⏰ ⏰
5.7	Offer relocation cards to pay moving expenses	💵	⏰ ⏰
5.8	Send payroll remittances by e-mail	💵 💵 💵	⏰ ⏰ ⏰
5.9	Post payroll remittances on the company intranet	💵 💵 💵	⏰ ⏰ ⏰
5.10	Allow online payroll remittance viewing only if employees use direct deposit	💵	⏰
5.11	Install ATMs at company locations	💵 💵	⏰
5.12	Charge intercompany fees for manual paychecks	💵	⏰
5.13	Use automated folders and sealers for paychecks	💵 💵	⏰ ⏰
5.14	Use IRS letter-forwarding service to deliver unclaimed paychecks	💵	⏰

1. **The checks must be printed.** Although it seems easy, it is all too common for the check run to fail, resulting in the manual cancellation of the first batch of checks, followed by a new print run.

2. **The checks must be signed** by an authorized check signer, who may have questions about payment amounts that may require additional investigation.

3. **The checks must be stuffed into envelopes** and then sorted by supervisor (because supervisors generally hand out paychecks to their employees).

4. **Then the checks are distributed,** usually with the exception of a few checks that will be held for those employees who are not currently on-site for later pickup. If checks are stolen or lost, the payroll staff must cancel them and manually issue replacements.

5. The person in charge of the bank reconciliation must track those checks that have not been cashed and follow up with employees to get them to cash their checks—there are usually a few employees who prefer to cash checks only when they need the money, surprising though this may seem.

In short, there are a startlingly large number of steps involved in issuing payroll checks to employees. How can we eliminate this work?

We can eliminate the printing and distribution of paychecks by using direct deposit. This best practice involves issuing payments directly to employee bank accounts. Besides avoiding some of the steps involved with issuing paychecks, it carries the additional advantage of putting money in employee bank accounts at once, so that those employees who are off-site on payday do not have to worry about how they will receive their money—it will appear in their checking accounts automatically, with no effort on their part. Also, there is no longer a problem with asking employees to cash their checks, because it is done automatically. Further, there is no longer any need to have an elaborate set of controls designed to store and track unused checks.

It can be difficult to get employees to switch over to direct deposit. Although the benefits to employees may seem obvious, some proportion of employees will prefer to cash their own checks or do not have bank accounts. To get around this problem, an organization can force all employees to accept direct deposit or do so only with new employees (existing employees are allowed to continue taking paychecks). If employees are forced to accept direct deposit, the company can arrange with a local bank to give them bank accounts or issue the funds to a debit card (as described in best practice 5.3, "Pay Employees through Payroll Cards"). Some companies also use raffles and other promotional devices to reward those employees who switch to direct deposit.

Another problem is the cost of this service. Banks typically charge $0.50 for each transfer made, which can add up to a considerable amount if there are many employees and/or many pay periods per year. However, banks also charge a fee to process checks, so the net cost of processing a direct deposit instead of a check is relatively low. Also, this problem can be reduced by shrinking the number of pay periods per year. In assessing the cost, one must factor in the time lost when employees go to the bank to deposit their checks; this factor alone makes the switch to direct deposit a cost-effective one.

Implementing direct deposit requires the transfer of payment information to the company's bank in the correct direct deposit format, which the bank uses to shift money to employee bank accounts. This information transfer can be accomplished either by purchasing an add-on to a company's in-house payroll software or by paying extra to a payroll outsourcing company to provide the service. Either way, there is an expense associated with starting up the service. If there is some trouble with finding an intermediary to make direct deposits, certain Web sites specialize in direct deposits. For example, *www.directdeposit.com* provides this service and even has upload links from a number of popular accounting packages, such as ACCPAC, DacEasy, and Great Plains.

Also, some paper-based form of notification still should be sent to employees, so that they know the details of what they have been paid. Thus, using direct deposit will not eliminate the steps of printing a deposit advice, stuffing it in an envelope, or distributing it. An alternative is to send remittance information to employees in an electronic format, which is dealt with in best practice 5.8, "Send Payroll Remittances by E-Mail."

Cost: 🏦   *Installation time:* 🕐🕐

5.2 Stop Delivering Checks to Employees at the Office

Some employees do not want to switch to being paid by direct deposit, because they want the security of being handed a real, live check on payday, hustling down to the bank, and converting it to cash. This is no different from having the funds electronically deposited in a bank account through direct deposit, but some people prefer to receive the physical check instead. The payroll staff has to track these people down in the company, verify their names, and hand over a check—a tedious and certainly nonvalue-added activity.

A simple way to eliminate the delivery of checks by hand and convince employees to switch to direct deposit is to mail checks to their homes on payday. By doing so, the payroll staff is removed completely from the check delivery business. Also, this best practice represents a control over check deliveries, because checks cannot be handed to the wrong person at the company. Last and best, putting checks into the mail introduces some uncertainty into the date on which they will arrive in employee mailboxes, making it possible that people who want a real check will have to wait an extra day before they have cash in their hands. Given this added level of uncertainty regarding payment, some companies have experienced a dramatic increase in the percentage of employees who voluntarily switch to direct deposit once check mailings commence.

The only downside to this approach is the cost of mailing all the checks, which is relatively minor.

Cost: 🖋️   Installation time: 🕰️

5.3 Pay Employees through Payroll Cards

Some companies employ people who, for whatever reason, either are unable to set up personal bank accounts or do not choose to. In these cases, they must take their paychecks to a check cashing service, which charges them a high fee to convert the check into cash. Not only is it expensive, but the check cashing service can have a long approval process. Also, employees will be carrying large amounts of cash just after cashing their checks, which increases the risk of theft. They also run the risk of losing their paychecks prior to cashing them. Thus, the lack of a bank account poses serious problems for a company's employees.

A good solution to this problem is to set up a debit card, called a payroll card, for any employees requesting one, and then shift payroll funds directly into the card. Doing this allows employees to pull any amount of cash they need from an ATM rather than the entire amount at one time from a check cashing service. The card also can be used like a credit card, so there is little need to make purchases with cash. Further, the fee to convert to cash at an ATM is much lower than the fee charged by a check cashing service. There is also less risk of theft through the card, because it is protected by a personal identification number (PIN). Employees also receive a monthly statement showing their account activity, which they can use to get a better idea of their spending habits. In addition to the monthly statement (which comes from the credit card issuer), the company still issues a payroll remittance advice to the employee through its regular payment procedures, which can be issued on paper or in an electronic format.

There are several other advantages to the payroll card. From the company's perspective, there is no longer a need to cut any type of paycheck for any reason, such as might previously have been the case for payments associated with awards, pay adjustments, or terminations. It also eliminates stop payment fees associated with lost checks and all internal costs associated with the ongoing reconciliation of a payroll bank account. Also, as is the case with direct deposit, the pay card keeps employees from leaving work to cash their checks and also allows them to be paid even if they are not in the office to collect payment. Finally, this practice completely eliminates escheatment, where an uncashed paycheck eventually must be remitted to the local state government as unclaimed property.

Using this card can be difficult for anyone who speaks English as a second language or who cannot understand ATM instructions. However, credit card companies offer multilingual customer service personnel, which reduces the severity of this problem.

The payroll card is rapidly becoming more common, though smaller payroll suppliers may not yet offer this function. Suppliers who are now advertising the payroll card capability include ADP, Ceridian, Ecount, FSV Payment Systems, Money Network, and PayMaxx.

Cost: 🖋 *Installation time:* 🕰 🕰

5.4 Offer Clear Cards to Employees

From time to time employees can find themselves in credit trouble, resulting in requests for payroll advances to their employers in order to meet pressing bill payments. A payroll advance is a time-consuming item to handle, because it involves the creation of a manual check, clearing the check on the next bank reconciliation, and offsetting the advance on the next paycheck.

An alternative to the payroll advance is to offer a "clear card" to employees. Under this approach, an employee pays for something with a credit card and then has the payment automatically deducted from his or her paycheck over the next two months, with no interest or late fees charged on the payment. Employees pay a yearly fee for this service; the employer pays no fee at all. The credit card provider installs the automatic linkage through the corporate payroll system to process payroll deductions, and does so free of charge. The card is available only to employees earning at least $20,000 per year and who have worked for the company at least six months. The credit limit on the card is 2.5% for those earning less than $75,000 per year, with a 4% limit for those earning above this amount.

Although the card has the clear advantage of offering a ready source of credit to employees who may otherwise not have available funds, it also can reduce their ready income if they constantly buy the maximum amount available to them, which may send them back to the company once again to ask for a payroll advance.

Cost: 💵   *Installation time:* 🕐🕐

5.5 Offer Prepaid Flexible Spending Account Cards

The human resources department handles the processing of flexible spending account (FSA) claims by employees. However, in smaller companies with no HR department, this labor-intensive chore falls on the payroll department. Under the FSA program, employees can opt to have a fixed amount withheld from their pay on a pretax basis each year, which they can then use for either medical or child care expenses (or both, if administered separately). The payroll staff collects expense receipts from employees, ensures that the expenses are valid under the FSA program, and then issues checks to the employees for the remitted amounts. Clearly, this is an exceedingly time-consuming process, and also requires the administration of a separate checking account and check stock.

An easy alternative is to offer prepaid flexible spending account cards to employees. The cards are charged with the full-year anticipated withholding for each employee, who then can use the money to pay for medical or child care expenses. The cards are restricted to merchants whose standard industrial classifications fall into either of these categories, so there is no chance that the cards will be misused. Although the card provider will charge a fee for these cards, the reduction in payroll staff labor is well worth the cost. Some payroll outsourcing suppliers, such as ADP, offer this as a complete outsourced solution; they handle the entire FSA program as well as the prepaid cards.

An excellent side benefit of the FSA card program is that their ease of use typically results in higher employee FSA deductions in subsequent years, which reduces the amount of their taxable income and therefore the level of matching social security payments that a company must incur.

Cost: 💵   *Installation time:* 🕐🕐

5.6 Offer Prepaid Incentive Cards

The payroll department does not like employee award programs, because it has to keep track of what dollar values were given to which employees through any of a multitude of corporate reward programs and then determine which rewards constitute reportable employee income.

Offering employees a prepaid incentive card is a good alternative. Under this approach, a company instructs its credit card provider to preload a debit card with the amount of a bonus payment intended for employees. The employees then can use this card to buy anything at any merchant location, rather than accepting a company award, which they may value considerably less. Alternatively, the company can control the card's use by restricting its acceptance to a smaller number of merchants. An excellent control over these cards is that the credit card provider will replace them if they are lost, with the remaining card balance included. Once used, the same cards can be used multiple times for different awards; the company can reload them with varying amounts of funds, depending on the award level being given. Banks offering this card include Chase, Citicorp, GE Corporate Payment Services, and First Banks.

This best practice is especially valuable to the payroll department, for if a company centralizes all of its incentives around a single card program of this type, the payroll staff can access a single monthly report to determine what compensation has been given to employees. Doing this makes it much easier to record the additional employee income in the payroll system, rather than attempting to track the value of other types of reward programs throughout the company.

Cost: 🖊️   *Installation time:* ⏲️ ⏲️

5.7 Offer Relocation Cards to Pay Moving Expenses

The payroll department can become involved in the complex task of tracking which travel expenses incurred by employees are to be reimbursed. The expense tracking and validation process is not the same as expense report auditing, because this task also requires spending up-front time with employees to discuss what expenses are allowable under company moving policies, possibly negotiating with employees for special move-related circumstances, and also working through the painful process of denying expense claims. In larger companies, doing this can be a daily chore, given the volume of employees being shifted among locations.

A simple approach for handling moving expenses is to issue a relocation debit card to each employee who is authorized to conduct a move. The card is charged with a specific amount of funds, which is all the employee is allowed to use for a specific move. The employee can charge only specific types of expenses to the card, which is designed to allow charges from certain types of move-related suppliers. Further, the expiration date of the card is set to coincide with the expected end of the employee move, so that no additional and unauthorized expenses can be charged to the card after that date. The payroll department can monitor the types and amounts of expenses as they are incurred by accessing the debit card Web site at any time. These expenses also can be summarized for all relocation cards issued, resulting in an excellent way to summarize moving expenses in each accounting period for posting to the general ledger. This approach is also useful for employees who do not need to submit a relocation expense report.

Given the cost to the card issuer of setting up this type of program, a company must have a large number of ongoing relocations to make this best practice cost-effective. Relocation cards are issued by MasterCard. More information about them can be found at *www.mastercardbusiness .com/mcbiz/corporate.*

Cost: 🖅   Installation time: 🕰 🕰

5.8 Send Payroll Remittances by E-Mail

A company may go to a great deal of trouble to install a direct deposit option in order to avoid sending checks to employees, only to find that it still must send a remittance advice, which lists the amounts paid and incidental data such as vacation or sick time earned. Because a company must send its employees some evidence of payment, it is difficult to avoid this distribution step.

A solution is to send remittances by e-mail, although there are some problems with this approach. One alternative is to have the payroll system compile a set of electronic messages after each payroll run, which then are loaded into a company's e-mail system for distribution to employees. Even though this seems like a relatively simple approach, there are a number of issues to overcome before it will work in a reliable manner. They are:

- *Custom programming.* The existing payroll software must be modified to allow for automated e-mail transmissions. The amount of programming required can be considerable, depending on the complexity of the software. Also, if the payroll software is a "canned" package that is upgraded periodically by a supplier, the custom programming may not work after the next upgrade, because the underlying software code will change.

- *Outsourced payroll.* If a company's payroll is outsourced to a supplier, then the payroll software is probably off-site, at the supplier's computer center. If so, it is highly unlikely that the supplier will agree to customize its payroll software to transmit e-mail messages.

- *Existing e-mail system.* It is impossible to send e-mail messages to employees if there is not a preexisting e-mail system in place to which all employees are connected. Such a system must be installed before one can consider e-mailing payroll remittances.

- *Employee access to computers.* An obvious problem is having employees, such as production workers, without ready access to computers on which they can check their e-mail. It is possible to avoid this issue by installing free-standing kiosks where all employees can check their e-mail. Another option is to send remittances to the e-mail addresses of employee supervisors, who can then print out the messages and distribute them. Yet another option is to send printed remittances only to those employees without access to e-mail.

- *Lost e-mail.* It is all too easy to press the "delete" button and see an e-mail message disappear forever. This can be a problem if the deleted e-mail happens to contain a payroll remittance. To avoid this problem, it may be necessary to allow employees to send an e-mail request to the payroll department to request either a new e-mail remittance or a hard copy of the remittance. It even may be possible to have employees contact the payroll database themselves to have a remittance printed out on a local printer, but this option carries the risk of having an employee discover the passwords for other employees and then print out their payroll remittances too.

- *Involuntary terminations.* This system breaks down if a payment is to an employee who has been terminated, because his or her company e-mail account will have been cancelled. In this case, the best approach is to issue a paper remittance advice to the employee.

Despite the number of complications that can arise when installing this best practice, it is still useful in many situations. It is of most use in such service industries as insurance, where nearly all employees have computers, and probably ill-advised in most production industries, where too few employees have ready access to this form of communication. Thus, the distribution of computers among employees is critical to the success of e-mailed payroll remittances.

Cost: 💵 💵 💵   *Installation time:* 🕐 🕐 🕐

5.9 Post Payroll Remittances on the Company Intranet

An alternative to proactively issuing electronic payroll remittances by e-mail (see best practice 5.8) is to post them on a company intranet site. By doing so, the company's only concern is making the pay information available. It no longer has to keep track of employee e-mail addresses, as there is no notification system in place. Instead, a schedule of posting dates is listed in the employee manual or a memo, and employees access their accounts on those dates to ascertain pay information. This approach tends to be popular with those employees having Web access, since they can access payroll information from anywhere—at work, at home, or on the road. It has the additional advantage of providing employees with pay information for any time period they want; an employee just selects from a list of previous pay dates to view the details for that paycheck.

Although this is a simpler approach than "pushing" payroll information to employees, there are still some issues to overcome:

- *Account security.* Each employee must be issued a user ID and password, and the intranet site must have high-quality security to prevent hackers from accessing key payroll information.
- *General employee access.* Although it is technically up to the employees to find their own access to the intranet site, the company should

recognize that some employees do not have access of any kind and provide terminals and printers at company locations to resolve this need.

- *Posting from payroll system.* The process of posting to the intranet site should be an automated one, and so likely will require a custom interface from the payroll system.

- *Outsourced payroll.* If a third-party supplier processes payroll, it will be difficult to obtain a data feed that can be posted to the intranet site. However, some payroll suppliers now offer feeds into their own Web-based systems where employees can access this information.

This approach also overcomes the problem of having to send a paper remittance to terminated employees as noted in best practice 5.8, because anyone can access the Web site, even people who have not been employees for a long time.

Cost: 💷 💷 💷   Installation time: 🕰 🕰 🕰

5.10 Allow Online Payroll Remittance Viewing Only If Employees Use Direct Deposit

Some employees have a strong preference for being handed an actual paycheck, walking it to a bank, and cashing it themselves, no matter how many inducements a company dangles before them to use direct deposit. Thus, there is always a small percentage of employees for whom the company must create a different paycheck handling process from everyone else.

A subtle inducement to make them switch to direct deposit is to implement an online payroll remittance system (as noted in best practice 5.9), but to allow viewing of the information only if an employee also has enrolled in the direct deposit program. Given the increasing dependence of society on access to electronic information, it is entirely possible that this added benefit will persuade a few more employees to make the switch to direct deposit. The lure will be especially great if additional features are added to the online payroll remittance program, such as allowing the viewing of multiple years of payroll information and access to an online W-2 form.

Cost: 💷   Installation time: 🕰

5.11 Install ATMs at Company Locations

Despite all the positive features of issuing pay cards to employees, employees who traditionally take their paychecks to a local check cashing service and then walk away with a large pile of cash still may find them difficult to accept.

A great way to gain employee acceptance of a switch to pay cards is to provide an automated alternative to the local check cashing store by installing an automated teller machine (ATM) at company locations. This gives employees the ability to convert their electronic pay into cash immediately. It also effectively gives them an implicit pay raise, because the company can set the ATM transaction fee at zero if it chooses to do so, whereas a check cashing service often charges 6% or more of the total paycheck amount. Further, having ready access to an ATM cuts down on employee time away from the office, which can be critical if they are involved in jobs such as manufacturing or customer service, where they can be away from their work only for short periods of time.

An ATM costs $3,000 to $6,000 to purchase outright, although larger, heavy-duty models used by banks can cost from $9,000 to $50,000. Obtaining a maintenance contract, which is typically about $300 per month, is advisable. ATMs also can be leased for a monthly fee. There are insurance costs associated with having a large amount of cash stored in the machine, although this cost can be reduced by having someone at the company load smaller amounts of cash into the ATM more frequently, rather than having a courier drive to each company location at infrequent intervals and load large amounts of cash into it. Each ATM also needs a dedicated power source and phone line. Finally, a payroll card holder's bank charges per-transaction fees to process each withdrawal transaction. Given the initial cost and ongoing transaction fees associated with this best practice, it is usually not a viable alternative unless a large number of employees are likely to use it.

ATMs can be obtained from a variety of ATM sales and service organizations, such as ATM Systems (*www.atmsystems.com*) and The ATM Warehouse (*www.atmwarehouse.com*).

Cost: 💵💵   *Installation time:* 🕰

5.12 Charge Intercompany Fees for Manual Paychecks

Some department managers go to great lengths to keep their staffs happy, including asking the payroll department to issue manual paychecks between regular pay periods. These manual checks may be for special bonuses, retroactive pay raises, and so on. Whatever the reason, the payroll staff must spend a considerable amount of time calculating taxes, writing the check, having it signed, and recording the check in the accounting system (which may require two entries: one in the payables system and another in the payroll system). Thus, writing a single manual check easily can consume 30 minutes of effort.

To mitigate the impact of manual paychecks, one can impose a substantial intercompany charge for each manual check written, perhaps in the range of $50 to $100 per check. This fee certainly will grab the attention of requesting managers and likely will make them think twice before requesting a manual check.

Cost: 🖋   *Installation time:* 🕐

5.13 Use Automated Folders and Sealers for Paychecks

When a company has a large number of employees, the payroll staff must fold paychecks, stuff them into envelopes, and seal the envelopes. This drudgery is not exactly the best use of the payroll staff's time, especially if the department is understaffed.

A cost-effective alternative for midsize to large companies is an automated folder and sealer machine. These devices fold letters, insert them into self-adhesive envelopes, and seal the envelopes. Examples of these manufacturers are Formax and VersaSeal. The VersaSeal approach is slightly different, using special paper that comes prelaminated with glue, which the equipment folds and seals, resulting in an envelope-free paycheck that is ready for mailing.

The price of these machines ranges from $4,000 to $45,000, based on the acceptable paper weight, hopper capacity, duty cycle, paper size, and processing speed of the equipment. For most companies, machines in the $4,000 to $6,000 range are perfectly adequate. Annual maintenance agreements should be obtained on any machine purchased, as the machines require periodic maintenance. A brief training program in the use of these machines also is recommended.

Cost: 💸💸   *Installation time:* 🕐🕐

5.14 Use IRS Letter-Forwarding Service to Deliver Unclaimed Paychecks

From time to time, employees will not claim their paychecks, usually because they have quit their jobs and moved on to other locations, leaving no forwarding address. This occurrence is common when an employee is attempting to avoid a garnishment situation. Whatever the reason, a company either must give the check to the employee or remit it to the local state government after some period of time as unclaimed property, which requires the extra burden of filling out unclaimed property forms.

A possible solution is to have the IRS obtain forwarding information for these employees. The IRS offers this service for free for 49 letters per calendar year. The instructions for contacting the IRS about this matter, excerpted from the IRS Web site, follow.

Step One. Prepare a cover letter directed to the IRS Disclosure Office for the local area where the requester is located. An example cover letter is shown in Exhibit 5.2. This cover letter should:

State why the IRS' assistance is being sought,

List the name(s), social security number(s), and (if available) last known address(es) of the individual(s) who cannot be located, and

Include the name and address of the person or organization to whom the IRS should send an acknowledgment letter (limited only to the acknowledgment of receipt of the sender's correspondence and an indication of whether or not the matter has been accepted into the letter forwarding program).

Exhibit 5.2   Cover Letter to the IRS Sample

Internal Revenue Service
Office of Disclosure
Address
City, State Zip

RE:

To Whom It May Concern:
We hereby request the use of the Internal Revenue Service Letter Forwarding Service. We currently represent [company name], which is attempting to forward paychecks to former employees. We are seeking to contact the XX [number less than 50] individuals listed below, who are entitled to receive these paychecks, but for whom we do not have addresses.

Enclosed is a list of the names, social security numbers, and last known addresses of the individuals we are seeking to contact. Also enclosed is a letter from us, directed to each of the missing individuals, advising of their rights to receive paychecks.

Thanking you in advance for your assistance in this matter.

Sincerely,

XXXXXXXXXXX
[appropriate officer or administrator]

Attachments:
List of Missing Former Employees
Letters Directed to Each of the Missing Former Employees

Step Two. Enclosed with the cover letter, include a letter (three pages or less) directed to the individual(s) who cannot be located. An example letter is shown in Exhibit 5.3. This letter should:

Advise the recipient of the reason for the letter,

Include instructions as to what the recipient should do to contact the sender, if he or she decides to respond,

Make clear that response to the sender's letter is completely voluntary on the part of the recipient, and

---

Exhibit 5.3   Letter Directed to Missing Participants Sample

Employee Name
Last Known Address
City, State Zip

Dear Mr./Ms. XXXXXXXXXXX:

According to our records, you have not received a paycheck you recently earned. Please contact us at the address or phone numbers listed above, so we can make arrangements to pay you the money you are owed.

*In accordance with current policy, the Internal Revenue Service has agreed to forward this letter because we do not have your current address. **The IRS has not disclosed your address or any other tax information** and has no involvement in the matter aside from forwarding the letter to you. Your response to this letter is completely voluntary.*

We are looking forward to hearing from you in the near future.

Sincerely,

XXXXXXXXXXX
Company Officer

Include the following disclaimer statement, "In accordance with current policy, the IRS has agreed to forward this letter because we do not have your current address. The IRS has not disclosed your address or any other tax information and has no involvement in the matter aside from forwarding this letter. Your response to this letter is completely voluntary."

Upon receipt of a valid request, the IRS Disclosure Office will search its records under the social security number provided and, if an address is found, forward the letter using an IRS envelope. If an address cannot be found or the letter is returned by the Postal Service as undeliverable, the letter will be destroyed. The requester will not be notified of this action. The law does not allow the IRS to provide the sender of such letter with the results of its efforts.

Step Three. Any third-party individual or organization requesting the use of the IRS letter-forwarding program on behalf of another party that is actually holding assets for a missing taxpayer must:

State in its cover letter to the IRS that it is acting on behalf of that other party, and

Present convincing documentation that he or she is acting as the authorized agent of an individual seeking to notify individuals who cannot otherwise be located that they are entitled to certain assets. In the case of a commercial locator service, written documentation must be provided by the service establishing it as the agent of the person controlling the assets (e.g., a letter from the controller of the assets to the IRS, delegating authority to the entity, or a copy of the letter from the controller of the assets to the commercial locator service engaging its services). However, no documentation is necessary when the letter to be forwarded contains instructions to the intended recipient to contact the controller of the assets directly.

If there is a need to contact more than 49 employees, the IRS charges a flat fee of $1,750, plus $0.01 per address search and $0.50 per letter forwarded. To make a request for forwarding of more than 49 notifications, write a request letter indicating the issue, the number of notifications to be forwarded, and a sample of the letter to be issued, and send it to this address:

> IRS, Director, Office of Disclosure
> CP: EX:D-Room 1603
> 1111 Constitution Avenue, NW
> Washington, DC 20224

The IRS will contact the company with a cost estimate and requirements for transmitting the information to the IRS.

An alternative is to use the letter-forwarding service of the Social Security Administration (SSA). The SSA charges a fee per letter forwarded. Its forwarding rules are:

- The fee should be paid with a check made payable to the Social Security Administration.

- A letter sent to the SSA for forwarding should be in a plain, unstamped, unsealed envelope showing only the missing person's name.
- The forwarding request should include the missing person's social security number or identifying information (date and place of birth, father's name, and mother's full birth name) to help the SSA find the social security number.
- Requests for letter forwarding should be sent to:

  Social Security Administration
  Letter Forwarding
  P.O. Box 33022
  Baltimore, MD 21290-3022

Cost: 💵   *Installation time:* ⏰⏰

6

Commission Calculations and Payments

This chapter addresses those 12 best practices having a direct impact on the calculation and payment of commissions. As noted in Exhibit 6.1, there are seven ways to either streamline or automate the calculation of commission payments, with the general emphasis being to simplify the commission structure on an ongoing basis. Next are three best practices dealing with the payment of commissions. The final two best practices deal with special items: error correction and minimizing the work associated with the month-end commission accrual.

Of the best practices noted in the exhibit, simplification of the commission structure is highly recommended, because complex structures can bedevil the payroll department, requiring constant reviews, error corrections, and recalculations. Also, the occasional use of a commission calculation audit should be considered; such audits can be useful in locating errors and especially in fixing the underlying problems that caused those errors, thereby achieving a more efficient commission calculation system.

The best practices noted in the exhibit are generally inexpensive, with the exception of the compensation management software; because this software is intended to automate highly complex commission systems, it may be worthwhile to point out to management that if they *really* want a complex commission system, then they will have to pay for it in the form of this software.

6.1 Simplify the Commission Structure

The bane of the payroll department is an overly complex commission structure. When there are a multitude of commission rates, shared rates, special

Exhibit 6.1   Commission Calculations and Payments Best Practices Summary

	Best Practice	Cost	Install Time
6.1	Simplify the commission structure	💵	⏰⏰⏰
6.2	Construct a standard commission terms table	💵	⏰
6.3	Periodically issue a summary of commission rates	💵	⏰
6.4	Calculate commissions automatically in the computer system	💵💵💵	⏰⏰
6.5	Install incentive compensation management software	💵💵💵	⏰⏰⏰
6.6	Pay commissions only from cash received	💵	⏰⏰⏰
6.7	Calculate final commissions from actual data	💵	⏰⏰⏰
6.8	Include commission payments in payroll payments	💵	⏰
6.9	Lengthen the interval between commission payments	💵	⏰⏰⏰
6.10	Periodically audit commissions paid	💵💵	⏰
6.11	Post commission payments on the company intranet	💵💵	⏰⏰
6.12	Avoid adjusting preliminary commission accrual calculations	💵	⏰

bonuses, and retroactive booster clauses, the commission calculation chore is mind-numbing and highly subject to error, which necessitates further analysis to fix. An example of such a system, based on an actual corporation, is for a company-wide standard commission rate, but with special increased commission rates for certain counties considered especially difficult regions in which to sell, except for sales to certain customers, which are the responsibility of the in-house sales staff, who receive a different commission rate. In addition, the commission rate is increased retroactively if later quarterly sales targets are met and is increased retroactively a second time if the full-year sales goal is reached, with an extra bonus payment if the full-year goal is exceeded by a set percentage. Needless to say, this company went through an endless cycle of commission payment adjustments, some of which were disputed for months afterward.

A simplification of the overall commission structure resolves this problem. For example, the previous example can be reduced to a single across-the-board commission rate, with quarterly and annual bonuses if milestone targets are reached. Although an obvious solution and one that can greatly reduce the work of the payroll staff, it is implemented only with the greatest difficulty because the sales manager must approve the new system, and rarely does so. The reason is that the sales manager probably created the convoluted commissions system in the first place and feels that it is a good one for motivating the sales staff. In this situation, the matter may have to go to a higher authority for approval, which irritates the sales manager. A better and more politically correct variation is to persuade the sales manager to adopt a midway solution that leaves both parties partially satisfied. In the long run, as new people move into the sales manager position, there may be more opportunities to simplify the commission structure.

Cost: 💵   *Installation time:* 🕑 🕑 🕑

6.2 Construct a Standard Commission Terms Table

Because salespeople may make the majority of their incomes from commissions, they have a great deal of interest in the exact rates paid on various kinds of sales. This interest can lead to many visits to the payroll clerk to complain about perceived problems with the rates paid on various invoices. Not only can such visits be stressful to the payroll clerk, who will be on the receiving end of some very forceful arguments, but they also are a waste of time, because that person has other work to do besides listening to sales staff arguments.

A reasonable approach that greatly reduces sales staff complaints is a commission terms table. It should specify the exact commission arrangement with each salesperson so there is absolutely no way to misconstrue the reimbursement arrangement. Once this table is set up, it can be distributed to the sales staff, who can refer to it instead of the payroll clerk. There will be the inevitable rash of complaints during the first few days after the table is issued; the sales staff will want clarification on a few key points, possibly requiring a reissuance of the table. However, once the table has been reviewed a few times, the number of complaints should dwindle rapidly. The only problem with this approach is that listing the commission deals of all the sales staff side-by-side on a single document will lead to a great deal of analysis and arguing by those sales personnel who think they are not receiving as good a commission arrangement. The best way to avoid this problem is to separate the table into pieces so each salesperson sees only that part of the table that applies to him or her. If this approach is followed, the number of inquiries and commission adjustments that the accounting staff must deal with will decline rapidly.

Cost: 🪙   *Installation time:* 🕐

6.3 Periodically Issue a Summary of Commission Rates

Even companies with a simplified and easily understandable commission structure sometimes have difficulty communicating this information to the sales staff. The problem is that the information is not readily available for sales personnel to see, and so they are always breeding rumors about commission alterations impacting their income. A continuing morale problem results, frequently resulting in needless inquiries to the payroll department.

The simple solution is to issue a summary of commission rates periodically. If management is comfortable with revealing the entire commission structure for all personnel, it can issue a commission table to the entire sales force. If not, it can issue a salesperson-specific commission listing. The table should be issued no less frequently than annually. A good way to present the commission information to a salesperson is to include it in the annual review, allowing each salesperson time to review it and ask questions about it. Also, the commissions table should be reissued and discussed with the sales force *every time* there is a change in the table, which keeps the payroll staff from having to explain the changes after the fact when the sales staff calls to inquire about the alterations. In short, up-front communications with the sales staff are a good way to keep the payroll department from having to answer inquiries about the commission information.

Cost: 🪙   *Installation time:* 🕐

6.4 Calculate Commissions Automatically in the Computer System

For many payroll clerks, the month-end calculation of commissions is not pleasant. Every invoice from the previous month must be assembled and reviewed, with notations on each one regarding which salesperson is paid a commission, the extent of any split commissions, and their amounts. Further, given the volume of invoices and the complexity of calculations, there is almost certainly an error every month, so the sales staff will be sure to pay a visit as soon as the commission checks are released in order to complain about their payments, which results in additional changes to the payments. The manual nature of the work makes it both tedious and highly prone to error.

The answer is to automate as much of the work as possible by having the computer system do the calculating. This way, the payroll clerk only has to scan through the list of invoices assigned to each salesperson and verify that each has the correct salesperson's name listed on it and the correct commission rate charged to it. To make this system work, there must be a provision in the accounting software to record salesperson names and commission rates against invoices, a very common feature on even less expensive accounting systems. However, if it does not exist, an expensive piece of programming work must be completed before this concept can be implemented. Then the accounting staff must alter its invoicing procedure so that it enters a salesperson's name, initials, or identifying number in the invoicing record for every new invoice. It is very helpful if the data-entry screen is altered to require this field to be entered, in order to avoid any missing commissions. Once this procedure is altered, it is an easy matter to run a commissions report at the end of the reporting period and then pay commission checks from it. This is a simple and effective way to eliminate the manual labor and errors associated with the calculation of commissions.

The main problem with using automated commission calculations is that it does not work if the commission system is a complex one. For example, the typical computer system allows for only a single commission rate and salesperson to be assigned to each invoice. However, many companies have highly varied and detailed commission systems, where the commission rates vary based on a variety of factors and many invoices have split commissions assigned to several sales staff. In these cases, only custom programming or a return to manual commission calculations will be possible, unless someone can convince the sales manager to adopt a simplified commission structure. This is rarely possible, because the sales manager probably created the complicated system and has no intention of seeing it dismantled.

Cost: 💵 💵 💵   *Installation time:* 🕐 🕐

6.5 Install Incentive Compensation Management Software

Commission tracking for a large number of salespeople is an exceedingly complex chore, especially when there are multiple sales plans with a variety of splits, bonuses, overrides, caps, hurdles, guaranteed payments, and commission rates. This task typically requires a massive amount of accounting staff time manipulating electronic spreadsheets and is highly error-prone. Several of the preceding best practices in this chapter are designed to *simplify* the commission calculation structure in order to reduce the amount of closing effort. However, an automated alternative is available that allows the sales manager to retain a high degree of commission plan complexity while minimizing the manual calculation labor of the payroll staff.

The solution is to install incentive compensation management software, such as is offered by Centiv, Synygy, and Callidus Software. This software is separate from the accounting software and requires a custom data feed from the accounting database, using the incoming data to build complex data tracking models that churn out exactly what each salesperson is to be paid, along with a commission statement. The best packages also allow for what-if modeling of different commission plan scenarios, as well as the construction of customized commission plans that are tailored precisely to a company's needs. Such plans also can deliver commission results to salespeople over the Internet. The trouble with this best practice is its cost. The software is expensive, and also requires consulting labor to develop a data link between the main accounting database and the new software. Thus, it is a cost-effective solution only for those organizations with at least 100 salespeople.

Cost: 💵 💵 💵   *Installation time:* 🕐 🕐 🕐

6.6 Pay Commissions Only from Cash Received

A major problem for the collections staff is salespeople who indiscriminately sell any amount of product or service to customers, regardless of the ability of those customers to pay. When this happens, the salesperson is focusing only on the commission resulting from the sale and not on the excessive work required by the collections staff to bring in the payment, not to mention the much higher bad debt allowance needed to offset uncollectible accounts.

The best practice that avoids this difficulty is to change the commission system so that salespeople are paid a commission only on the cash received from customers. This change instantly will turn the entire sales force into a secondary collection agency, because they will be very interested in bringing in cash on time. They also will be more concerned about the creditworthiness of their customers and will spend less time selling to customers that have little realistic chance of paying.

Three problems make this a tough best practice to adopt:

1. As it requires salespeople to wait longer before they are paid a commission, they are markedly unwilling to change to this new system.

2. The amount they are paid will be somewhat smaller than what they are used to receiving, because inevitably there will be a few accounts receivable that will never be collected.

3. Because of the first two issues, some of the sales staff will feel slighted and may leave the company to find another organization with a more favorable commission arrangement. Accordingly, the sales manager may not support a change to this type of commission structure.

A tougher variation is not to pay commissions at all if invoices go over 90 days old, on the grounds that the commission system should push the sales staff to collect as soon as possible. This variation is least effective when commissions are quite small in comparison to the base pay of the sales staff and most effective when commissions make up a large proportion of a salesperson's pay.

A problem directly related to the accounting systems (and not the intransigence of the sales department!) is that because commissions now are paid based on cash received, there must be a cash report to show the amounts of cash collected from each customer in a given time period, in order to calculate commissions from this information. Most accounting systems already contain this report; if not, it must be programmed into the system.

Cost: 🪙   *Installation time:* 🕐 🕐 🕐

6.7 Calculate Final Commissions from Actual Data

It is common to pay departing salespeople immediately for the commissions they have not yet received, but which they should receive in the next commission payment. Unfortunately, the amount of this commission payment often is a guess, because some sales have not yet been completed and orders have not even been received for other potential sales on which a salesperson might have been working for months. Accordingly, the typical salesperson's hiring agreement usually contains a complicated formula that pays out a full commission on completed sales, a partial one on orders just received, and perhaps even a small allowance on expected sales for which final orders have not yet been received. The work required to complete this formula is highly labor-intensive and frequently inaccurate, especially if an allowance is paid for sales that may not yet have occurred (and that may never occur).

A better approach is to restructure the initial sales agreement to state that commissions will be paid at the regular times after employee termination until all sales have been recorded. The duration of these payments may be several months, which means that the salesperson must wait some time to receive full compensation. The payroll staff benefits from not having to waste time on a separate and highly laborious termination calculation. Instead, they take no notice of whether a salesperson is still working for the company and just calculate and pay out commissions in accordance with regular procedures.

There are three problems with this approach:

1. If the sales calculation is made automatically in the computer system, sales probably will be assigned to a new salesperson as soon as the old one has left, requiring some manual tracking of exactly who is entitled to payment on which sale during the transition period.

2. If a salesperson is fired, most state laws require immediate compensation within a day or so of termination. Although the initial sales agreement can be modified to cover this contingency, one should check first to see if the applicable state law will override the sales agreement.

3. This type of payout usually requires a change to the initial employee contract with each salesperson; the existing sales staff may have a problem with this new arrangement because they will not receive payment so quickly if they leave the company. A company can risk irritating the existing sales staff by unilaterally changing the agreements, but it may want to try the more politically correct approach of grandfathering the existing staff and applying the new agreement only to new sales employees.

In short, delaying the final commission payment runs the risk of mixing up payments between old and new salespeople, may be contrary to state laws, and may be applicable only to new employees. Despite these issues, implementing this best practice still is a good idea, even though several years may pass before it applies to all of the sales staff.

Cost: 💵   *Installation time:* 🕐 🕐 🕐

6.8 Include Commission Payments in Payroll Payments

If a company has a significant number of sales personnel, the chore of issuing commission payments to them can be a significant one. The taxes must be compiled for each check and deducted from gross pay; the checks must be cut or a wire transfer made; and, for those employees who are out of town, other special arrangements may be needed to get the money to them. Depending on the number of checks, issuing commission payments can interfere with the smooth functioning of the payroll department.

A simple but effective way to avoid this problem is to roll the commission payments into the regular payroll processing system. By doing so, the payroll calculation chore is completely eliminated, once the gross commission amounts are approved and sent to the payroll staff for processing. The system will calculate taxes automatically, issue checks or direct deposits, or mail them to employees, depending on the distribution method the regular payroll system uses. This process completely eliminates a major chore.

There are two problems with this best practice.

1. The commission payment date may not coincide with the payroll processing date, which necessitates a change in the official commission payment release date. For example, if the commission is always paid on the fifteenth day of the month, but the payroll is on a biweekly schedule, the actual pay date certainly will not fall on the fifteenth day of every month. To fix this issue, the commission payment date in the example could be set to the first payroll date following the fifteenth of the month.

2. By combining a salesperson's regular paycheck with the commission payment, the combined total will put the employee into a higher pay bracket, resulting in more taxes being deducted (never a popular outcome). This issue can be resolved either by setting employee deduction rates lower or by separating the payments into two checks in the payroll system in order to drop the payee into a lower apparent tax bracket.

As long as these issues are taken into account, merging commissions into the payroll system is a very effective way for the payroll staff to avoid calculating and cutting separate commission checks.

Cost: 💵   *Installation time:* 🕐

6.9 Lengthen the Interval between Commission Payments

Some commissions are paid as frequently as once a week, although monthly payments are the norm in most industries. If there are many employees receiving commission payments, this level of frequency results in a multitude of commission calculations and check payments over the course of a year.

It may be possible in some instances to lengthen the interval between commission payments, reducing the amount of commission calculation and paycheck preparation work for the payroll department. This best practice is useful only in a minority of situations, however, because the commissions of many sales personnel constitute a large proportion of their pay, and they cannot afford to wait a long time to receive it. However, in some instances salespeople receive only a very small proportion of their pay in the form of commissions. In this situation, it makes little sense to calculate a commission for a very small amount of money and is better to do it only at a longer interval, perhaps quarterly or annually. Although it can be used only in a few cases, this best practice is worth considering.

Cost: 💵   *Installation time:* 🕐🕐🕐

6.10 Periodically Audit Commissions Paid

Given the complexity of some commission structures, it comes as no surprise that the sales staff is not always paid the correct commission amount. This is particularly true during transition periods, when payment rates change or new salespeople take over different sales territories. When this happens, there is confusion regarding the correct commission rates to pay on certain invoices or whom to pay for each one. The usual result is that some overpayments go uncorrected; the sales staff will peruse commission payments closely to make sure that underpayments do not occur, so this is rarely a problem. In addition, there is a chance that overpayments are made on a regular basis, because those salespeople on the receiving end of this largesse are unlikely to report it.

The best way to review commissions for errors is to schedule a periodic internal audit of the commission calculations. This review can take the form of a detailed analysis of a sampling of commission payments or a much simpler overall review of the percentage of commissions paid out, with a more detailed review if the percentage looks excessively high. Any problems discovered through this process can result in some retraining of the payroll clerk, an adjustment in the commission rates paid, or a reduction in the future payments to the sales staff until any overpayments have been deducted fully from their pay. This approach requires some time on the part of the internal audit staff but does not need to be conducted very frequently and so is not an expensive proposition. An occasional review is usually sufficient to find and correct any problems with commission overpayments.

Cost: 💵 💵   *Installation time:* 🕐

6.11 Post Commission Payments on the Company Intranet

A sales staff whose pay structure is heavily skewed in favor of commission payments rather than salaries probably will hound the payroll staff at month-end to see what their commission payments will be. This comes at the time of the month when the payroll staff is trying to close the accounting books and so increases its workload at the worst possible time of the month. However, by creating a linkage between the accounting database and a company's Internet site, it is possible to shift this information directly to the Web page where the sales staff can view it at any time, without involving the valuable time of the payroll staff.

There are two ways to post the commission information. One is to wait until all commission-related calculations have been completed at month-end and then either manually dump the data into an HTML (HyperText Markup Language) format for posting to a Web page, or else run a batch program that does so automatically. Either approach will give the sales staff a complete set of information about their commissions. However, this approach still requires some manual effort at month-end (even if only for a few minutes while a batch program runs).

An alternative approach is to create a direct interface between the accounting database and the Web page, so that commissions are updated constantly, including grand totals for each commission payment period. By using this approach, the payroll staff has virtually no work to do in conveying information to the sales staff. In addition, sales personnel can check their commissions at any time of the month and call the payroll staff with their concerns right away—this is a great improvement, because problems can be spotted and fixed at once, rather than waiting until the crucial month-end closing period to correct them.

No matter which method is used for posting commission information, a password system will be needed, because this is highly personal payroll-related information. There should be a reminder program built into the system, so that salespeople are forced to alter their passwords on a regular basis, thereby reducing the risk of outside access to this information.

Cost: 💵 💵   *Installation time:* 🕐 🕐

6.12 Avoid Adjusting Preliminary Commission Accrual Calculations

The controller frequently hounds the payroll manager early each month for a commission accrual for commissions earned during the past month but not yet paid. This information is a necessary part of the financial statements.

If a company has several salespeople who frequently share commissions through a variety of split commission deals, it is highly likely that the initial commission calculations put together by the payroll staff will allocate commissions incorrectly; a second iteration is required before there is a correct allocation of the commission expense by person. However, the process of determining the correct allocation is a slow one, often requiring the input of the sales manager, who may not be available at the precise point during the financial statement closing period when his or her input is required. Thus, developing a proper commission allocation can interfere with the closing process significantly, causing undue pressure on the payroll manager.

A simple way to avoid this problem is not to worry about it, because the initial total commission accrual is probably very close to what the final commission accrual will be after all allocations have been made among the sales staff—in short, the commission on each sale stays the same, with the only issue being who receives the payment. Thus, there is no need to adjust the initial commission accrual, resulting in a fast delivery of the accrual to the controller and far less pressure on the payroll manager.

Cost: *Installation time:* 🕰

7

Payroll Outsourcing

This chapter describes seven best practices related to various aspects of the payroll and benefits administration functions. They are presented in order of applicability by company size, with the first four services available to all companies and the final three being cost-effective only for large organizations.

The first best practice presents the general concept of payroll outsourcing, while the second one hones in on the best outsourcing alternative for today's payroll department—using a Web-based system. This should be considered the core of a potentially all-encompassing outsourcing strategy, which can be expanded to include benefits administration, W-2 form creation and electronic delivery, as well as unemployment claims management (although the last two options require large headcounts to be cost-effective). A more specialized alternative is to link hosted payroll processing

Exhibit 7.1   Payroll Outsourcing Best Practices Summary

	Best Practice	Cost	Install Time
7.1	Outsource the payroll function	💵	🕐 🕐
7.2	Use Web-based payroll outsourcing	💵	🕐 🕐
7.3	Outsource benefits administration to a payroll supplier	💵 💵	🕐 🕐
7.4	Outsource tax filings	💵	🕐 🕐
7.5	Outsource W-2 form creation and delivery	💵	🕐
7.6	Link hosted payroll processing to an ERP system	💵 💵	🕐 🕐
7.7	Outsource unemployment claims management	💵 💵	🕐 🕐

to an in-house enterprise resource planning (ERP) system, although again this option is only available for larger companies.

The outsourcing opportunities noted here generally take some time to implement and will be more successful if implemented in a paced, sequential manner, rather than all at once. By doing so, the payroll manager can be assured of a careful roll-out of systems with proper attention having been paid to employee training as well as data conversion to the new systems.

7.1 Outsource the Payroll Function

A typical in-house payroll department has many concerns. Besides the task of issuing paychecks, it may have to do so for many company locations, where tax rates differ, employees are paid on different dates, and tax deposits must be made to state governments by different means (e.g., direct deposit, bank deposit, or mail) and W-2 forms must be issued to all employees at the beginning of each year. Of all these issues, the one carrying the heaviest price for failure is a government tax deposit—missing such a payment by a single day can carry a large penalty that rapidly accumulates in size. All of these problems and costs can be avoided by handing over some or all portions of the payroll function to an outside supplier.

Payroll is one of the most commonly outsourced company functions. There are several good reasons for this:

- *Tax remittances.* A supplier pays all payroll taxes without troubling the company. The savings from avoiding government penalties for late tax payments will, in some cases, pay for the cost of the payroll supplier.

- *Multilocation processing.* The supplier usually can process payroll for all company locations; several suppliers are based in all major cities, so they can handle paycheck deliveries to nearly any location. Other smaller suppliers get around not having multiple locations by sending checks via overnight delivery services. Either approach works very well.

- *Direct deposit.* Suppliers can deposit payments directly into employee bank accounts, which is something that many in-house payroll systems, especially the smaller ones, cannot do.

- *Check stuffing.* The time-consuming task of stuffing checks into envelopes is one that many suppliers will handle, thereby freeing up the internal staff for less mundane work.

- *Reporting.* Suppliers also provide a wide array of reports, usually including a report-writing package that can address any special reporting needs. Once again, many smaller in-house payroll systems lack a report-writing package, so this can be a real benefit.

- *New hire reporting.* Most states require a company to report to them whenever a new employee is hired, so they can determine if that person can be garnished for some outstanding court claim. Suppliers sometimes provide this service for free, because they can easily batch all new hires for all their customers and forward this information electronically to the state governments.

- *Expert staff.* Suppliers are staffed with a large team of experts who know all about the intricacies of the payroll process. They can answer payroll questions over the phone, provide specialized or standard training classes, or come out to company locations for hands-on consulting.

- *Cost.* A study commissioned by ADP and independently conducted by PricewaterhouseCoopers shows that the total cost of outsourcing can be 30% less than the cost of having in-house payroll processing. The wide array of benefits has convinced thousands of companies to switch to an outsourced payroll solution.

- *Backups.* Although not usually considered a significant reason to outsource, suppliers back up their payroll systems at least daily, so there is minimal risk of lost payroll data.

- *Other services.* As noted in the other best practices in this chapter, some suppliers offer additional services, especially in the areas of benefits administration, 401(k) plans, and unemployment compensation management, that allow a company to outsource not only much of its payroll work, but also a great deal of its human resources functions as well.

Suppliers offering some or all of the functionality just noted include ADP, Inc. (*www.adp.com*), Ceridian (*www.ceridian.com*), Paychex, Inc. (*www.paychecx.com*), and PayMaxx, Inc. (*www.paymaxx.com*).

However, before jumping on the outsourcing bandwagon, a few reasons for *not* using a payroll supplier must be considered. One is that outsourcing can be more expensive than an in-house solution in some situations (despite the finding of the ADP study noted above), because the supplier must spend funds to market its services as well as make a profit—two items that an in-house payroll department does not include in its budget. A supplier usually will sell its services to a company by offering an apparently inexpensive deal with a small set of baseline services and then charge high fees for add-on services, such as direct deposit, check stuffing, early check deliveries, report-writing software, and extra human resources functionality. As long as a company is well aware of these extra fees and budgets them into its initial cost-benefit calculations, there should be no surprises later on, as more supplier services are added and fees continue to mount.

The other main problem with outsourcing is that the payroll database cannot be linked to a company's other computer systems. Because its payroll data usually are located in a mainframe computer at an off-site supplier location, it is difficult to create an interface that will allow for electronic user access to payroll data. The best alternative (although it is a poor one) is either to keypunch the most important data in a company payroll database from payroll reports printed by the supplier or to download data from the supplier's computer. Because of this missing database linkage, a number of larger companies prefer to keep their payroll-processing work in-house. For an alternative available only to large companies, see best practice 7.6, "Link Hosted Payroll Processing to an ERP System."

In short, there are many good reasons for a company to outsource its payroll function to a qualified supplier. The only companies that should not do so are those that are highly sensitive to the cost of payroll processing or those that must link their payroll data to other company databases.

Cost: 💲   *Installation time:* ⏲ ⏲

7.2 Use Web-Based Payroll Outsourcing

Payroll processing has been the most common accounting function to outsource for many years. However, such outsourcing suffers from several deficiencies, such as having to submit information to the payroll supplier only on certain days, or (if the amount of data is minimal) waiting for a supplier representative to call, so the information can be conveyed over the phone. In addition, any information that is verbally conveyed to the supplier runs the risk of being incorrect, because an additional person is involved in the data entry. Yet another problem is that the supplier typically will run the payroll in a batch-processing run that evening and then deliver the completed payroll to the company one or two days later, which is the earliest point at which the accounting staff knows the exact amount of its payroll liability (information it needs for cash management purposes).

To get around these problems, it is now possible to process a payroll over the Internet. Doing this involves accessing a supplier's Web site, entering payroll and time card information on the spot, and gaining access to fully processed payroll information either immediately or within no more than an hour. This approach also allows one to enter payroll information at any time of the day or night and to avoid additional data-entry problems that are caused by the supplier using an extra data-entry person.

A particularly fine benefit to this approach is that no new software must be installed on a computer in the accounting department. Such software is needed for traditional outsourced payroll processing, where the data entry is conducted by an accounting clerk into a local computer and then uploaded to the supplier through a modem or broadband connection. This software may be incompatible with other operating or application software on the computer, generally requires that the computer be reserved for payroll use (since it contains sensitive information), must be updated as the supplier issues new software versions, and costs money—payroll suppliers charge several hundred dollars to give participating companies the "privilege" of using it.

In addition, large organizations can eliminate the computer on which the payroll software used to run. For very large organizations, doing this may result in the elimination of a mainframe-size computer, with all its attendant personnel, maintenance, and support costs.

The main downside to Web-based payroll processing is that it can be difficult to access or process if there is a poor Internet connection (increasingly unlikely as the use of broadband connections spread). Also, as is the case for any outsourced payroll, the payroll information is kept separate from other accounting information in the company's central database, so it is difficult to combine payroll information with other types of information for reporting purposes.

This type of payroll processing is offered by many suppliers, including PayMaxx, Inc. (*www.paymaxx.com*), Ceridian Corp. (*www.ceridiansmallbusiness.com*), Genesys (*www.genesys-soft.com*), and the Emerging Business Services division of Automatic Data Processing, Inc. (*www.ebs.adp.com*).

Cost: ✐   Installation time: ▨ ▨

7.3 Outsource Benefits Administration to a Payroll Supplier

Although benefits normally are administered through a separate human resources department, the payroll staff can become involved in two ways:

1. If the company is so small that both functions are combined into the payroll department, or
2. If the payroll staff must handle benefit-related deductions and the disposition of the deducted funds.

The latter situation occurs in nearly all companies, because a growing trend is to shift a greater proportion of benefit costs to employees through deductions. If there are a large number of different benefit providers, this can result in more time being spent on deduction tracking than on timekeeping.

Outsourcing benefits administration to the same company that provides a company's payroll services is an ideal way to improve the situation. For example, by shifting 401(k) withholding to the payroll supplier, the payroll staff no longer has to track the amount of 401(k) funds to transfer to the third-party plan administrator, because this is now done automatically by the payroll supplier. The same approach applies to flexible spending accounts (FSAs), which can be administered by the payroll supplier. An added benefit here is that a company can eliminate a bank account, which usually is kept separately to track withheld FSA funds. Further, employees usually can manage changes to their benefit packages online by accessing Web portals maintained by the payroll supplier, thereby removing benefits data entry from the payroll staff's list of responsibilities. Payroll suppliers that provide benefits services include ADP, Inc. (*www.adp.com*), Ceridian (*www.ceridian.com),* and PayMaxx, Inc. (*www.paymaxx.com*).

Outsourcing benefits administration tends to be a better approach than acquiring software that conducts the same functions. The reason is that one can pay for only those aspects of a benefits outsourcing program that are most necessary, whereas acquiring a commercial software program will result in the acquisition and payment of ongoing maintenance on *all* the functionality of that software, which likely contains a great deal more than is needed.

If there is a downside to the consolidation of many services with a single supplier, it is the company's dependence on that organization for a long period of time; shifting services that have been consolidated away from a supplier can be difficult (or at least inconvenient). Consequently, it is useful to closely examine the payroll and benefits administration supplier's financial status, local operations staff, and operating procedures to ensure that there is a close fit that will likely result in a comfortable long-term relationship.

Cost: 💵 💵   *Installation time:* 🕐 🕐

7.4 Outsource Tax Filings

The primary risk in the payroll department is of making an incorrect tax calculation or remittance, either of which can result in hefty government fines. Further, issuing hundreds and potentially thousands of tax returns to government entities in a single year (depending on the number of employees and their distribution throughout the country) is extremely time-consuming. Consequently, the area of tax filings is the core area that many payroll managers are most interested in outsourcing, even while retaining all other aspects of the payroll function.

Several suppliers offer a tax filing service that includes filings for state disability and unemployment insurance, W-2 forms, and amended returns, while also filing all quarterly and annual payroll tax returns and responding to tax agency inquiries on behalf of the company. To perform these functions, suppliers require a data feed from the in-house payroll system that details the payroll liability in each reporting period. Because the data feed must be customized to the requirements of the supplier, a small amount of programming work may be required.

Examples of suppliers offering tax filing services include Ceridian (*www.ceridian.com*), Federal Liaison Services (*www.flsinc.com*), Genesys Software Systems (*www.genesys-soft.com*), Humanic Solutions (*www.humanic.com*), and PayMaxx, Inc. (*www.paymaxx.com*).

Cost: 💵   *Installation time:* 🕐 🕐

7.5 Outsource W-2 Form Creation and Delivery

Shortly after year-end, the payroll department comes under pressure from those employees who suspect they have a tax refund coming and want their W-2 forms as soon as possible in order to obtain the refund. However, and especially in larger companies with thousands of employees, printing and mailing W-2 forms can be a major chore that tends to be delayed. Also, some employees inevitably lose their W-2 forms, resulting in more work by the payroll staff in reissuing replacement forms.

A cost-effective solution for larger companies is to send their W-2 data by a data feed to the W-2 eXpress product of TALX (*www.talx.com*), which can issue electronic or faxed W-2 forms to those employees who opt for this service or issue traditional paper-based W-2 forms to all remaining employees. Under the electronic delivery approach, employees can access the supplier's Web site, enter their social security number and a PIN number, and have immediate access to their W-2 forms for the past four years in PDF format. It is also possible for employees to download W-2 information directly into some of the more common tax filing software packages.

If W-2 information is incorrect, the service also allows for either subsequent data feeds containing W-2c information or online manual updates to the previously submitted information.

This approach also allows the payroll manager to monitor employee W-2 usage, as well as call up copies of W-2 forms for individual employees.

There are two issues with outsourcing W-2 form creation and delivery:

1. It generally is cost-effective only for companies having at least 10,000 employees.
2. A data feed to the supplier must be arranged. Although suppliers have interfaces with the most common payroll software systems, designing an export file compatible with the supplier's data requirements may require some programming.

Cost: 💵   Installation time: 🕲

7.6 Link Hosted Payroll Processing to an ERP System

Large companies that have made the decision to switch to a company-wide enterprise resources planning system may face the conundrum of finally having complete access to all possible employee information in one database but not being willing to undertake responsibility for payroll processing and tax remittances. However, manually converting this information for entry into the standard payroll screens of most outsourcing suppliers requires a massive amount of manual data entry time that also will likely result in some data entry errors.

If a company is large enough, an alternative is the Enterprise Payroll system offered by ADP. Under this approach, ADP will create an interface from the corporate ERP system, so it can access payroll information from the ERP system automatically without manual intervention. All subsequent payroll processing tasks can be handled through a Web browser. This approach gives a larger company all the advantages of the traditional outsourcing solution, while still yielding complete access to all payroll data within its own database for ad hoc querying purposes.

Given the cost of the interface design, installation, and testing, this solution is available only to larger corporations.

Cost: 💵 💵   *Installation time:* 🕰 🕰

7.7 Outsource Unemployment Claims Management

Even if a company has separate human resources and payroll departments, the payroll staff is regularly forced to shoulder the burden of responding to unemployment claims, because the required information is contained within the payroll database. Doing this can be a major chore, especially if the payroll staff also is required to represent the company with the state's assigned unemployment case officer when former employees contest the company's assertions about their unemployment status.

Unemployment claims administration can be shifted to an outside service, which takes over responsibility for all claims filings, from initial claims through final disposition. These organizations summarize all claims on a secure Web site, where the payroll manager can readily determine the status of claims and related hearings. Also, because they have large staffs who deal with nothing but unemployment claims, their knowledge base is considerable. An example of this service is the UC eXpress product of TALX Corporation (*www.talx.com*).

This service is not cost-effective for smaller businesses. TALX estimates that its services are viable only for organizations having at least 500 employees or 1,000 claims per year.

Cost: 💵 💵   *Installation time:* 🕰 🕰

8

Payroll Management

This chapter contains 28 best practices related to the concept of payroll management. Because this topic is so broad, the chapter contains several subcategories of best practices including basic department management, process improvement, payroll systems, customer service, and miscellaneous topics. A summary of the payroll systems, including a ranking of their costs and installation time, is shown in Exhibit 8.1.

The first cluster of five best practices relates to basic documentation of payroll processes and staff training issues. First on the list is creating a policies and procedures manual, which is extremely useful for training new employees, serving as the launching point for a process review, and also as a training tool for a new manager, who can use this documentation task as a learning tool for what goes on in the department. Next in line is the issuance of an activities calendar, which is an excellent tool for coordinating department activities. Finally, the use of a training program, cross-training, and certifications are good ways to improve the knowledge base and indirectly the retention level of the payroll department.

The second cluster of nine best practices addresses process improvement. A good way to understand department problems is to construct a reporting tool that summarizes transaction errors. Eliminating transaction backlogs allows the payroll staff more time to investigate these errors. Another key error-reduction technique is to centralize tasks with as few individuals as possible, so there are fewer task handoffs between staff members. Two other useful ways to increase process efficiency are to reduce the number of payroll cycles by lengthening pay periods and to avoid off-cycle payrolls as much as possible.

The third cluster of best practices contains seven best practices related to the improvement of payroll systems, either through database consolidation or automated tie-ins to the existing database. Key areas of improvement

---

Exhibit 8.1   Payroll Management Best Practices Summary

Best Practice	Cost	Install Time
Basic Department Management		
8.1 Create a policies and procedures manual	💵	🕐🕐
8.2 Issue activity calendars to all payroll employees	💵	🕐
8.3 Create a payroll training program	💵💵	🕐🕐
8.4 Implement cross-training	💵	🕐🕐
8.5 Require payroll certifications	💵	🕐🕐🕐
Process Improvement		
8.6 Continually review transaction errors	💵	🕐
8.7 Eliminate all transaction backlogs	💵💵	🕐
8.8 Process nonpay-affecting changes during off-peak periods	💵	🕐
8.9 Implement process centering	💵💵	🕐🕐
8.10 Minimize payroll cycles	💵	🕐🕐🕐
8.11 Minimize off-cycle payrolls	💵	🕐
8.12 Store upcoming transactions in dated folders	💵	🕐
8.13 Create a year-end payroll processing checklist	💵	🕐
8.14 Simplify the pay structure	💵	🕐🕐🕐
Payroll Systems		
8.15 Link the payroll and human resources databases	💵💵💵	🕐🕐🕐
8.16 Merge the payroll and human resources departments	💵💵💵	🕐🕐🕐
8.17 Link payroll changes to employee events	💵💵💵	🕐🕐🕐
8.18 Link the 401(k) plan to the payroll system	💵	🕐🕐🕐
8.19 Make electronic child support garnishment payments	💵	🕐🕐🕐
8.20 Install manager self-service	💵💵💵	🕐🕐🕐
8.21 Automate employment and income verification requests	💵💵	🕐🕐

Exhibit 8.1 (Continued)		
Best Practice	**Cost**	**Install Time**
Customer Service		
8.22 Publish answers to frequently asked questions on an intranet site	💵	⏰
8.23 Operate a payroll help desk	💵 💵	⏰ ⏰
8.24 Implement a service-level agreement with other departments	💵	⏰ ⏰
8.25 Designate intermediaries to maintain contact with fellow service providers	💵	⏰
Miscellaneous Topics		
8.26 Use the Common Paymaster rule to reduce payroll taxes	💵	⏰
8.27 Review the impact of voluntary unemployment contributions	💵	⏰
8.28 Acquire the unemployment experience rating of a predecessor organization	💵	⏰ ⏰

here include linking the payroll and human resources databases, adopting activity triggers based on employee events, and installing manager self-service, although all three involve major programming investments. A lower-cost best practice that measurably improves department efficiencies is to link the 401(k) plan to the payroll system; this is more achievable if both processes are handled by the same payroll outsourcing supplier. For additional best practices involving large computer systems, refer to Chapter 9, "Payroll Systems."

The payroll department is not just a cost center—it is also one of the most important services provided to employees. Accordingly, a cluster of four best practices deal with customer service, including the use of a payroll help desk, publishing answers to frequently asked questions (FAQs) on the company intranet site, and formulating service-level agreements.

Finally, three best practices do not fall into any of the preceding categories. They all relate to cost reduction activities, including the reduction of payroll taxes and two ways to reduce unemployment taxes.

Many of the best practices presented in this chapter are core improvements that should be considered prior to the implementation of the more specialized topics covered in other chapters, because they relate to the fundamental ordering of work within the payroll department. For a more thorough treatment of the correct sequence in which best practices should be implemented, see Chapter 13, "Best Practices Implementation Plan."

Basic Department Management

8.1 Create a Policies and Procedures Manual

An unorganized payroll department is inefficient, suffers from a high transaction error rate, and does not complete its work products on time. Although training, cross-training, and calendars of events (as described in best practices 8.3, 8.4, and 8.2 respectively) will contribute to a more structured environment, one of the best ways to create a disciplined payroll department is to create and maintain a policies and procedures manual.

This manual should list the main policies under which the department operates. These are the key issues that confront each functional area and usually are limited to just a few pages. Anything longer probably indicates an excessive degree of control or some confusion in the difference between a policy and a procedure.

A good example of a policy is one that sets a boundary for an activity. A procedure, however, defines the precise activities that take place within the boundaries the policies create. A procedure is usually sufficient to use as a guideline for an employee who needs to understand how a process works. When combined with a proper level of training, the policies and procedures manual is an effective way not only to increase control over the payroll department, but also to enhance its efficiency.

There are some pitfalls to consider when constructing the manual, as well as for maintaining and enforcing it. They are:

- *Not enough detail.* A procedure that does not cover activity steps in a sufficient degree of detail is not of much use to someone who is using it for the first time; it is important to list specific forms used, computer screens accessed, and fields on those screens in which information is entered, as well as the other positions that supply information for the procedure or to which it sends information. It also may be helpful to include a flowchart, which some people find is more understandable than text.

- *Not reinforced.* A procedures manual does not do much good if it is immediately parked on a remote shelf. Instead, it should be made an integral part of all training programs and included in periodic discussions regarding the updating and improvement of key processes. Only through constant attention will the manual be used to the fullest extent.

- *Too many procedures.* A common problem is that the manual is never released because the payroll manager is determined to include a procedure for every conceivable activity the department will ever encounter. However, the main principle to follow is that the manual must be issued soon, so it is better to issue it quickly with procedures that cover the bulk of payroll activities and to address the remaining procedures at a later date. This approach gets the key information to those employees who need it the most, and does so quickly.

The single most important factor in the success of a policies and procedures manual is an active payroll manager. This person must reinforce the use of the manual with the staff so it is not simply ignored as a one-time report gathering dust on a shelf. Only through continual attention by the entire staff will the manual become the foundation of how all key payroll processes are completed.

Cost: 🖋️   *Installation time:* 🕐 🕐

8.2 Issue Activity Calendars to All Payroll Employees

Disorganization is the bane of any payroll department. The payroll department is responsible for consistently completing the same tasks, day after day and year after year, with a great deal of reliability. If the employees cannot organize themselves properly so key tasks are completed on time, the entire function can fall into disarray, resulting in payrolls and tax remittances not being completed on time. Clearly, some instrument of organization must be found.

The calendar is an excellent tool for straightening out the timing of accounting work. One can create a calendar on the computer, either with a scheduling software package or an electronic spreadsheet, and load it with all of the tasks that must be completed each day. An example of such a calendar is shown in Exhibit 8.2. Although some employees are naturally well

Exhibit 8.2   Sample Monthly Activities Calendar

Sunday	Monday	Tuesday	Wednesday	Thursday	Friday	Saturday
1	2 Commission Calculation Tax Deposit Remit Garnishments Remit 401(k) Funds Review Time Sheets	3	4 Verify Life Insurance Verify Medical Enrolls Verify Deductions	5 Department Meeting	6	7
8	9 Overtime Report Payroll Processing Review Time Sheets	10 Create Journal Entry	11 Verify Life Insurance Verify Medical Enrolls Verify Deductions	12 Department Meeting	13 Issue Paychecks	14
15	16 Overtime Report Tax Deposit Remit Garnishments Remit 401(k) Funds Review Timesheets	17	18 Update Vacation Schedule	19 Department Meeting	20	21
22	23 Overtime Report Review Time Sheets	24 Payroll Processing	25 Create Journal Entry Payroll Report to CEO	26 Department Meeting	27	28
29	30 Overtime Report Issue Paychecks Review Time Sheets Calculate Metrics Update Procedures					

organized and will already have it in place, many others will be in desperate need of this simple organizational tool. The best way to distribute these calendar schedules is to keep the schedules for all employees in a single location, update them at the end of each month, and have a staff meeting to distribute them so the payroll manager can emphasize all calendar changes. It is then a simple matter to refer to copies of all employees' calendars each day and follow up with them to ensure that they are completing the scheduled tasks.

Cost: 🖋️   *Installation time:* ⏰

8.3 Create a Payroll Training Program

The efficiency and effectiveness of a payroll department are based on many factors, but a crucial one that all too many payroll managers ignore is training. Many managers simply assume that their staffs have acquired all the knowledge they need in college and in subsequent work experience and need no further training of any kind. This belief is based on the erroneous assumptions that all payroll practices are the same, no matter where employees work, and employees can be neatly swapped between jobs and organizations with no additional training of any kind. Over the long term, this erroneous idea can have a major impact on the payroll staff, for these reasons:

- *Computer-specific knowledge.* There are many payroll software packages in use, all with their own quirks and foibles. Each of these packages requires special training before employees will fully comprehend how to use them more effectively, as well as (perhaps more important) what *not* to do, because some systems require expert usage to run properly.

- *Lack of management training.* Payroll is not just clerical—it requires an excellent knowledge of how to manage processes in a multitude of functional areas, frequently including employees in outlying locations. Without proper management training, the department will almost certainly suffer from gross inefficiencies and errors.

- *Lack of process training.* The payroll function deals with processes, especially the periodic processing of paychecks. All employees in this department must have a clear knowledge of exactly how these processes work so they can process information through them most efficiently, as well as make modifications that will further increase the level of efficiency. Although some of this knowledge can be gleaned through many years of experience, it is best to cut short this interval through a training program that imparts both the fundamentals and the detailed steps involved in all key organizational processes.

- *Lack of training for advanced positions.* Although employees may be adequately trained in their existing jobs, this does not mean that they are in any way prepared to take over positions higher in the payroll hierarchy. Without the necessary training to prepare them for these positions, employees may become frustrated and leave for other organizations willing to provide the training for more advanced and higher-paying jobs.

- *Payroll rule changes.* Local, state, and federal governments constantly are changing how payroll transactions are completed and reported, resulting in a multitude of regulatory changes. Anyone who has not received formal training in these changes within the past few years must be trained in all rules updates; those who have not been trained in a decade or more will require comprehensive retraining.

All of these reasons sum up strongly in favor of a detailed and prolonged training program for the entire payroll department, covering such areas as software, processes, new payroll regulations, industry-specific issues, and general management training.

The best way to set up a training program is for one to make a list of all positions in the payroll department and determine the training strengths and weaknesses of every person occupying those positions. Then one must assemble a master list of all possible training, with the required training for each person noted on the list. An example of such a list is shown in Exhibit 8.3, which lists the training program for a variety of software modules in a payroll software package.

Employees usually must be forced to complete their scheduled training, because they find that there is not enough time in the midst of their other activities to fit it in. To avoid this issue, the payroll manager should schedule a monthly review of completed training to ensure that all employees are meeting their training goals. Also, training goals should be included in the targets that employees must meet each year in order to be given pay raises or bonuses. Further, the internal audit staff also may schedule an occasional review of all training records to ensure that employees are indeed

Exhibit 8.3   Sample Master Training Schedule

Software Task Training	Abdullah, B.	Bronson, C.	Cavez, T.	Dingle, D.
Entering bonus data	8/1/0X		3/12/0X	
Setting up a direct deposit	8/1/0X	5/5/0X		6/20/0X
Deleting a direct deposit	8/15/0X	5/5/0X		
Handling direct deposit error codes			3/12/0X	
Entering garnishment data	8/15/0X			7/14/0X
Canceling a garnishment order		6/28/0X	3/12/0X	7/14/0X
Setting up a new employee		6/28/0X	3/31/0X	
Terminating an employee	9/30/0X		3/31/0X	
Reviewing timekeeping information	9/30/0X			7/14/0X
Adjusting timekeeping information	9/30/0X	2/16/0X	5/1/0X	7/14/0X
Printing W-2 forms	9/30/0X	2/16/0X	5/1/0X	

completing their training work and not falsely reporting training hours that never happened. When combined, all of these measures will ensure a thorough and comprehensive training program that will improve employee knowledge.

Cost: 💰💰   *Installation time:* ⏰⏰

8.4 Implement Cross-Training

A number of crucial payroll activities will cause a significant amount of disturbance within an organization if they are not completed on time, every time. The greatest risk is that only one person knows how to process transactions. If that person leaves the organization or is incapacitated for any reason, there can be a serious system failure that will quickly bring the entire organization to a grinding halt.

The solution is to implement cross-training using other payroll department employees. By doing so, there is far less risk that mission-critical activities will not be performed in a reliable manner, which greatly reduces the chance that any key activity will not be completed on time.

A listing of required training elements should be available on a schedule of key activities. The payroll manager should identify those personnel who are most qualified to act as backups, put them through the training regimen, and ensure that they receive continual retraining, so they can easily step into the needed jobs. A small pay hike for those employees receiving cross-training will ensure their enthusiastic participation in this system. The key factor to remember is that training alone does not make for a good backup person—only continual hands-on practice under the direct tutelage of the person who is currently responsible for the work will ensure that this best practice will succeed.

The only people who ever oppose this best practice are those who are currently in charge of mission-critical functions. They feel more valuable if they are the only ones who can complete a task and will feel less useful if someone else also can do the work. Overcoming this problem requires a great deal of tact and diplomacy. Sometimes they continue to be hostile to the concept and must be removed to other positions while their replacements figure out the system without any support at all. These are difficult alternatives, but must be followed through if there is to be an adequate degree of cross-training in key functional areas.

Cost: 🖋️   *Installation time:* 🕑 🕑

8.5 Require Payroll Certifications

Payroll is a profession, and as such it involves knowledge of a massive number of constantly changing rules and regulations. However, the payroll department tends to be staffed by a small number of knowledgeable managers and a large number of clerks who are well trained only in very specific areas of payroll processing. The result tends to be a stagnant department, because the clerks are encumbered by their lack of knowledge in devising better ways to process transactions and by their lack of knowledge of payroll regulations.

A good way to improve this situation is to require all payroll staff to obtain payroll certifications, or at least to have them in order to qualify for pay raises or promotions. Two certifications worth obtaining are the Fundamental Payroll Certification (FPC) and the Certified Payroll Professional (CPP), both available through the American Payroll Association (APA). Its Web site is *www.americanpayroll.org*. The FPC is designed for those beginner-level employees needing a basic level of knowledge of the payroll function; the CPP is a much more intensive program involving both an experience requirement and the completion of several APA courses prior to taking the test. Payroll managers should encourage employees to complete all requirements for the CPP, as it yields a substantially higher level of payroll knowledge that encompasses payroll systems, taxation, management, and regulatory compliance. It is also likely that employee morale will improve through this program, because management is clearly making an investment in its staff.

Cost: 💵   *Installation time:* 🕐 🕐 🕐

Process Improvement

8.6 Continually Review Transaction Errors

The payroll department is one of those unfortunate departments whose errors are highly visible, even though no one seems to notice when transactions are processed in an error-free manner. The trouble is that payroll is a highly sensitive area, revolving as it does around paying employees, so even a small number of errors tend to appear magnified in the eyes of the workforce. Nonetheless, payroll managers tend to play down errors, behavior that simply leaves the same underlying transactional problems lurking in the background, waiting to rise up and cause more errors in the future.

The solution is to draw up a formal list of errors each month and go over them with the payroll staff. By creating a formal system for addressing issues and finding ways to ensure that they do not happen again, there is a good chance that errors will decline over time. It is also useful to track error types on a trend line, to see which errors keep recurring. These are the ones to which the most management attention should be directed, so that appropriate controls can be implemented to reduce their incidence.

Cost: 💵   *Installation time:* ⏰

8.7 Eliminate All Transaction Backlogs

The payroll staff gets into serious trouble when it develops a permanent backlog of payroll transactions, usually in the areas of employee database updates or timekeeping compilations. When a backlog arises, key payroll information may not be updated for some time, resulting in payments to the wrong addresses, late pay updates, improper tax withholdings, and the like. Further, transaction backlogs tend to create piles of paperwork in which other documents can be lost, resulting in extra search time to locate needed materials.

A crucial best practice is to eliminate these backlogs, usually by allocating extra staff time to do them. Once the piles of paperwork are eliminated, the payroll manager can focus on increasing levels of training and process improvement to reduce the number of people required to keep the backlog from recurring. The main point is to make transaction entries at the time of initial occurrence as easy as possible, so there is no need for the payroll staff to delay the data entry task.

If the department has a highly variable amount of transaction volume, some backlog may reappear in periods of high activity, although this problem can be avoided by planning to hire part-time workers to assist the regular staff at such times.

Cost: 💵 💵   *Installation time:* ⏰

8.8 Process Nonpay-Affecting Changes During Off-Peak Periods

The payroll staff usually is buried by an enormous pile of payroll changes that it inputs into the payroll system during a relatively small part of the month. These changes include alterations to addresses, marital status, direct deposit information, deduction amounts, hours worked, overtime, and so on. Most of these items must be entered prior to the next payroll, which creates a major work bottleneck within the payroll department.

There are several ways to make a minor reduction in the size of this bottleneck. One is set aside all payroll changes that do not have a direct impact on an employee's pay, such as name changes and address changes, and process them only during slow periods in the department work cycle. Another is to enforce a cutoff date by which all payroll changes can be submitted to the department, thereby giving the payroll staff several days in which to enter the changes prior to actually running the next payroll. Changes impacted by this policy can include deductions, withholding amounts, marital status, and salary rates. By making these changes, only information about hours worked should be left for last-minute data entry. A likely side benefit is a reduction in the number of payroll errors, because the payroll staff is less rushed to enter changes in the payroll system.

Cost: 💵   *Installation time:* 🕰️

8.9 Implement Process Centering

A major problem at many companies is the inordinate amount of time it takes to complete a process. For example, insurance companies are famous for spending many weeks to review an insurance claim and issue a payment check, even though the total amount of work required is under an hour. The long time period from the beginning to the end of the process usually is due to the number of transfers between employees. For example, the insurance branch office may forward a claim to an insurance adjuster, who passes it along to a manager if the amount exceeds a set level, or who hands it off to another person who checks to see if the claim may be fraudulent or if the claimant has an unusually long history of claims, then moves the paperwork to another person who issues checks, and then returns the entire packet to the insurance branch office. Insurance is just an example—companies invest a shocking amount of time in moving paperwork between a multitude of employees. A related problem is that paperwork can be lost when it is moved between employees. Further, it is difficult to pin blame on anyone when a transaction is completed improperly because there are so many people involved in the process. Thus, spreading work among too many people opens a virtual Pandora's box of troubles.

The solution is called *process centering*. Its underlying principle is to cluster as many work tasks for a single process as possible with a single person. By doing so, there are fewer transfers of documentation, which reduces the amount of time lost during these movements, while at the same time eliminating the risk that paperwork will be lost. Further, employees have much more complete and fulfilling jobs because they see a much larger part of the process and have a better feeling for how the entire process works. And best of all for a company, the time needed to complete transactions drops drastically, sometimes to less than 10% of the time previously needed.

The main problem with process centering is employee resistance. In this reengineering best practice, the old process is ripped up and replaced with an entirely new work flow, which makes employees nervous about their jobs, or if they will even have a job when the changes are complete. Accordingly, they usually are not pleased with the prospect of a new system and resist vigorously, or at least are of minimal assistance. Only excellent communications and a strong commitment by top management to completing the project will make this best practice operational, given the likely level of resistance to it.

Cost: 💸 💸   Installation time: ⏰ ⏰

8.10 Minimize Payroll Cycles

Many payroll departments are fully occupied with processing some kind of payroll every week, and possibly even several times in one week. The latter situation occurs when different groups of employees are paid for different time periods. For example, hourly employees may be paid every week, and salaried employees may be paid twice a month. Processing multiple payroll cycles eats up most of the free time of the payroll staff, leaving it with little room for cleaning up paperwork or researching improvements to its basic operations.

All of the various payroll cycles can be consolidated into a single, company-wide payroll cycle. By doing so, the payroll staff no longer has to spend extra time on additional payroll processing, nor does it have to worry about the different pay rules that may apply to each processing period—instead, everyone is treated exactly the same. To make payroll processing even more efficient, it is useful to lengthen the payroll cycles. For example, a payroll department that processes weekly payrolls must run the payroll 52 times a year, whereas one that processes monthly payrolls only does so 12 times per year, which eliminates 75% of the processing that the first department must handle. These changes represent an enormous reduction in the payroll-processing time the payroll staff requires.

Any changes to the payroll cycles may be met with opposition by the organization's employees. The primary complaint is that the employees have structured their spending habits around the timing of the old pay system and that any change will not give them enough cash to continue those habits. For example, employees who currently receive a paycheck every week may have a great deal of difficulty in adjusting their spending to a paycheck that arrives only once a month. If a company were to switch from a short to a longer pay cycle, it is extremely likely that the payroll staff will be deluged with requests for pay advances well before the next paycheck is due for release, which will require a large amount of payroll staff time to handle. To overcome this problem, pay cycles can be increased incrementally, perhaps to twice a month or once every two weeks, and employees also can be told that pay advances will be granted for a limited transition period. By making these incremental changes, the associated amount of employee discontent can be reduced.

The payroll manager should review the prospective change with the rest of the management team to make sure that it is acceptable to them. They must buy into the need for the change, because their employees also will be impacted by it, and they will receive complaints about it. This best practice requires a long lead time to implement, as well as multiple notifications to the staff about its timing and impact on them. It is also useful to go over the granting of payroll advances with the payroll staff, so that they are prepared for the likely surge in requests for advances.

Cost: 💸   *Installation time:* 🕐🕐🕐

8.11 Minimize Off-Cycle Payrolls

Every time the payroll department creates an off-cycle payroll, a great deal of additional work is required: reviewing open transactions, summarizing hours worked, entering and cross-checking entries in the payroll software, running and reviewing a payroll register, printing checks, and distributing them. Off-cycle payrolls are needed when significant processing errors in a normal payroll cycle call for an extra processing run, or when a department manager wants to issue a separate set of paychecks to staff, usually for bonuses.

There are a few ways to ensure that off-cycle payrolls are kept to a minimum. One is to create an interdepartmental charge that is applied whenever a manager demands that an extra payroll cycle be completed for the staff. If this fee is sufficiently large, most managers probably will consent to having extra payments added to the next regularly scheduled payroll cycle instead. Another alternative is to require high-level approval, perhaps from the chief financial officer, to initiate an off-cycle payroll; this option also tends to keep managers from demanding such payrolls.

If payroll errors are causing extra payroll cycles to be run, then the payroll manager should delay minor error adjustments until the next regularly scheduled payroll cycle, only using a special cycle for inordinately large errors. The payroll manager should consider in advance what types of errors will require an off-cycle payroll and enter these decision points in the department procedures manual, so the payroll staff is aware of when they need to create off-cycle payrolls and when they can be avoided.

Cost: *Installation time:*

8.12 Store Upcoming Transactions in Dated Folders

Many payroll transactions must be repeated in multiple future payroll cycles or will be repeated only during specific future cycles. Given the large number of payroll cycles that the typical payroll department processes each year, it can be difficult to ensure that all transactions are completed and that they are done during the correct cycles.

A simple, nontechnical answer is the use of dated folders. At the beginning of each year, a staff person should create a series of dated folders, one for each payroll cycle throughout the year. A paper copy of the transaction that must be completed during that cycle should be stored in each folder. These transactions can include deductions for personal purchases, garnishments, pay rate changes, return dates from maternity leave, and so on. To ensure that repetitive transactions are completed in every required cycle, one should make copies of these transactions and put one in every folder representing a cycle when some action is required.

Cost: 🖙   *Installation time:* 🕰

8.13 Create a Year-End Payroll Processing Checklist

The payroll function has so many tasks to attend to at the calendar year-end that it is difficult *not* to forget some key tasks. When this happens, the payroll staff usually pays for it later in the new year with reissued paychecks or W-2c forms, altered tax remittances, and so on. All these corrections take more time to research and fix than if the tasks had been completed properly at the appropriate time. Also, a number of tasks must be completed to prepare for the next payroll year, or else the payroll staff will find itself scrambling to make retroactive changes later in the new year.

The solution is to create a year-end payroll processing checklist. If a company outsources its payroll, its supplier probably maintains such a list and would be happy to hand over a copy. Another approach is to gradually build up a checklist over several years, including additional items as the payroll staff becomes aware of new legal requirements or changes in company benefits that result in more tasks to complete. The next list includes some of the more common closing tasks to consider:

- Final year-end payroll tasks:
  - Report the amount of employee income associated with group term life insurance exceeding $50,000.
  - Withhold for and report on taxable fringe benefits.
  - Withhold for and report on third-party sick pay.
  - Verify that all manual paychecks cut during the year have been included in the payroll database.
  - See if full-year pension plan deductions exceeded the allowable limit.
  - Schedule a year-end bonus payroll.
  - Create W-2 forms.
- Preparing for new payroll year:
  - Verify the amount of unemployment tax rates and associated wage limits.

- Determine if a voluntary unemployment contribution should be made to reduce the upcoming unemployment tax rate for the new year.
- Notify employees to review their W-4 forms.
- Update employee withholdings based on revised W-4 forms.
- Notify employees of unused flexible spending account deductions.
- Verify the need for special income or deduction accumulators.
- Verify the amount of standard employee deductions for the new year.
- Reset pension plan deduction levels for the new year.
- Purge terminated employees from the payroll database.
- Verify that upcoming payroll processing dates do not fall on a weekend.
- Issue a schedule of payroll processing dates for the new year to employees.

Cost: 💸   *Installation time:* 🕐

8.14 Simplify the Pay Structure

A typical company has a relatively simple pay structure, where salaried employees earn the same amount every paycheck and hourly employees earn a set amount per hour, with additional overtime in accordance with state law. However, there are more complex situations where the pay calculation requires considerably more effort to complete and is much more likely to be incorrect. These situations usually are driven by union labor agreements, where employees are paid different amounts if they switch pay grades, substitute for someone in a different pay grade, switch to a different shift, work on a Saturday versus a Sunday, and so on. Not only do these pay structures make payroll calculations more difficult, but they also eliminate from consideration a number of commercial timekeeping systems that otherwise might be available to a company trying to improve its payroll processing efficiency. Instead, the company is forced to use legacy systems that were designed specifically to handle the pay structure; even when these systems are in place, changes to the pay structure require additional programming changes to the software. In short, a complex pay structure appears designed to reduce the efficiency of the payroll department.

The solution is to gradually negotiate changes to the pay structure that are specifically designed to increase the ease of payroll calculations. This solution may encompass bargaining over several successive union agreements before a sufficiently simplified arrangement is achieved, so consider this best practice to be a work in progress for multiple years.

Cost: ✎   *Installation time:* 🕰 🕰 🕰

Payroll Systems

8.15 Link the Payroll and Human Resources Databases

The payroll database shares many data elements with the human resources (HR) database. Unfortunately, these two databases usually are maintained by different departments—payroll for the first and HR for the second. Consequently, any employee who makes a change to one database, such as an address field in the payroll system, must then walk to the HR department to have the same information entered again for other purposes, such as benefits administration or a pension plan. Thus, there is an obvious inefficiency for the employee who must go to two departments for changes, while the payroll and human resources staffs also duplicate each other's data entry efforts.

An alternative is to tie the two databases together. This can be done by purchasing a software package that automatically consolidates the two databases into a single one (see Chapter 9, "Payroll Systems").

The considerable cost of buying and implementing an entirely new software package will exceed the cost savings obtained by consolidating the data by a great deal. A less costly approach is to create an interface between the two systems that automatically stores changes made to each database and updates the other one as a daily batch program. Creating this interface still can be expensive, because it involves a reasonable amount of customized programming work. Consequently, this best practice is an expensive proposition and usually is done only when both computer systems are being brought together for more reasons than a simple reduction in data-entry work.

If the two databases are consolidated into a single system, the initial conversion of data from both originating systems into it can be a major operation. Someone must design an automated conversion program that shifts the old data into the format used by the new system, merge the data from both databases, and then import them into the new system. Also, the new system probably will have a number of processing steps, screens, and online forms that differ from the systems being replaced, so both the payroll and HR staffs will require training just before the "go live" date for the new system.

Cost: 💵 💵 💵   *Installation time:* ⏰ ⏰ ⏰

8.16 Merge the Payroll and Human Resources Departments

A natural extension of the preceding best practice is to not merge just the payroll and HR databases, but to merge the two departments. By doing so, a company can handle all employee-related transactions from one location: hiring, pay raises, benefits, retirement plans, termination, exit interview, Consolidated Omnibus Budget Reconciliation Act (COBRA) paperwork, and so on. This approach can increase employee morale by concentrating all their interactions with a single group of people, rather than forcing them to contact two separate departments, each with different databases that may not contain the same information.

The problems with this best practice are mostly political. The HR department may report to a vice president of HR, while the payroll manager generally reports to the controller. In order to merge the departments, someone's reporting relationship will have to change, which can cause considerable bickering. In addition, merging policies and procedures, as well as databases, can consume a considerable amount of time. Further, if department employees are asked to gain a thorough understanding of both human resources *and* payroll issues (useful for providing a single point of contact to company employees), a comprehensive department-wide training program must be implemented. Thus, this best practice tends to be a long-term project.

Cost: 💵 💵 💵   *Installation time:* ⏰ ⏰ ⏰

8.17 Link Payroll Changes to Employee Events

Many payroll changes must be made when certain events occur in an employee file. Many of these changes are never made, because the payroll staff is so busy with the standard, daily processing of information that it has no time to address them, or because the payroll staff does not possess enough knowledge to link the payroll changes to the employee events. For example, when an employee gets married, this should trigger a change in that person's W-4 form, so that the amount of taxes withheld will reflect those for a married person. Automation can create many of these linkages. Some examples of automatic procedures are:

- As soon as an employee reaches the age of 55, the system issues a notification to the pension manager to calculate the person's potential pension, while also notifying the employee of his or her pension eligibility. These notifications can be by letter, but a linkage between the payroll system and the e-mail system could result in more immediate notification.

- As soon as an employee has been with the company for 90 days, his or her period of probation has been completed. The system then should automatically include the employee in the company's dental, medical, and disability plans and include deductions for these amounts in the person's paycheck. Similarly, the system can automatically enroll the employee in the company's 401(k) plan and enter the deductions in the payroll system. Because these^ pay changes may come as a surprise to employees, the system also should generate a message to them, detailing the changes made and their net payroll impact.

- When the company is informed of an employee's marriage, the computer system generates a notice to the employee that a new W-4 form should be filled out, while also sending a new benefit enrollment form, in case the employee wishes to add benefits for the spouse or any children. Finally, a notification message can ask the employee if he or she wants to change the beneficiary's name on the pension plan to that of the spouse.

- When an employee notifies the company of an address change, the system automatically notifies all related payroll and benefit suppliers, such as the 401(k) plan administrator and health insurance provider, of the change.

- When a new employee is hired, the system sends a message to the purchasing department, asking that business cards be ordered for the person. Another message goes to the information systems department, requesting that the appropriate levels of system security be set up for the new hire. Yet another message goes to the training department, asking that a training plan be set up for the new employee.

Many of these work-flow features are available on high-end payroll and human resources software packages. However, this software costs more than $1 million in most cases, and so is well beyond the purchasing capability of many smaller companies. An alternative is to customize an existing software package to include these features, but the work required will be expensive. Accordingly, these changes should be contemplated only if there are many employees, which would result in a sufficient volume of savings to justify the added expense.

Cost: 💸 💸 💸   Installation time: 🕐 🕐 🕐

8.18 Link the 401(k) Plan to the Payroll System

A common activity for the payroll staff is to take the 401(k) deduction information from the payroll records as soon as each payroll cycle is completed, enter it into a separate database for 401(k) deductions, copy this information onto a compact disc (CD), and send it to the company's 401(k) administration supplier, who uses it to determine the investment levels of all employees as well as for discrimination testing. The data-entry process involved can be lengthy if there are many employees, and it is certainly not a value-added activity when the core task simply is moving data from one database to another.

The best way to avoid retyping 401(k) payroll deductions is to link the payroll system directly into a 401(k) plan. This is done by outsourcing the payroll processing function to a supplier who also offers a 401(k) plan. A good example of this is Automated Data Processing (ADP), which offers linkages to a number of well-known mutual funds through its payroll system. When a company uses ADP's payroll and 401(k) services, a payroll department can record a 401(k) payroll deduction for an employee just once; ADP then takes the deduction and automatically moves it into a 401(k) fund, with no additional bookkeeping required from the payroll staff. For those companies with many employees, this best practice can represent a significant reduction in the workload of the payroll staff.

There are two problems with this best practice:

1. A company must outsource its payroll function to a supplier that offers 401(k) administration services, which the payroll manager may not be willing to do.
2. Converting to the new 401(k) plan may cause difficulty. To do so, all employees in the old plan must be moved to the new plan. The associated paperwork may be great enough to make the transition not worthwhile; also, the 401(k) administrator may require a separation fee if the company is terminating its services inside of a minimum time interval, which may involve a small penalty payment.

These issues should be considered before switching to a centralized payroll and 401(k) processing system.

Cost: 🖉   *Installation time:* 🕑 🕑 🕑

8.19 Make Electronic Child Support Garnishment Payments

The payroll departments of larger companies having multiple employees may process a seemingly unending stream of child support garnishment payments. Each garnishment may last for years, resulting in a cumulative total of well over 100 separate payments just on a single garnishment order.

A good way to avoid the labor-intensive processing of these payments is to initiate electronic Automated Clearing House (ACH) payments to the local state agency that processes child support garnishments. Doing this requires calling the local agency to determine its specific electronic payment formatting needs and the bank account to which payments must be made. A list of the local agency contact names for each state is located at *www.acf .hhs.gov/programs/cse/newhire/employer/contacts/eftedi_statecontacts .htm*, a site administered by the Financial Management Service (a bureau of the Department of the Treasury). This list also notes which states provide free software for making electronic payments. An overview of the electronic payments program also is available at the Financial Management Service Web site (*http://fms.treas.gov/csp/index.html*).

The basic payment transaction is to transmit an "Entry Detail Record," containing payment information, as well as an 80-character "Addenda Record," which provides additional information about the specific payment being made. Getting the contents of these records exactly right may require several months of effort, and the process must be duplicated for each state (each of which may have different information requirements).

The advantages of making electronic child support payments include the complete elimination of all mailing costs and related mailing delays, increased accuracy of transmitted information, and better assurance that payments will be made on time and in the correct amounts. However, the effort required to set up electronic payments does not make this a cost-effective alternative if there are only a few child support payments to be made each month.

Cost: 💵   *Installation time:* 🕐🕐🕐

8.20 Install Manager Self-Service

A considerable amount of payroll staff time is occupied by the setup and deletion of employees from the payroll database, as well as by the recording of payroll events, such as employee pay raises, transfers, and employee leave situations. Usually a local manager fills out paperwork pertaining to these events and forwards them to the payroll department, which keypunches the information into the payroll system. This work flow can result in lost or delayed paperwork as well as incorrect data entry. If the events being entered pertain to employee pay raises, an error also is likely to result in boisterous contacts by the affected employee.

An elegant solution is to create an intranet portal through which local managers can enter all of this information themselves, with no need for any data entry by the payroll staff. Because most managers already have access to a computer terminal, generally no additional computer hardware must be acquired.

The efficiency improvement resulting from this best practice for the payroll staff is obvious. However, in order to prevent staff from immediately converting to error-correction mode for all the errors being made by local managers through the new payroll intranet site, there are a number of enhancements to consider when building the site:

- *Install data limit checkers.* Managers inadvertently may enter incorrect information that is patently false, such as a $1,000,000 salary, by not entering a decimal place. The data-entry system can include a number of data-limit checkers that will reject data automatically unless it falls within a tight parameter range.

- *Require transaction-specific approvals.* If a manager wants to give an employee an inordinately large pay raise, the system should bring this raise to the attention of the payroll staff or an upper-level manager, who must approve it before the payroll database is updated with the new information.

- *Issue warnings to affected departments.* When a manager enters an employee termination into the computer system, this act should trigger a message to the human resources department, which may want to conduct an exit interview. Similarly, the 401(k) plan administrator needs to know about the termination in order to send plan termination documents to the former employee; the same goes for the health plan administrator, who must mail out a packet of COBRA information. A number of similar notifications are needed at the point of initial hire.

Thus, the manager data-entry system is not really a simple interface. It must review input data, issue notifications and warnings, and generally take over the roll of an experienced payroll clerk to ensure that employee transition data is correctly handled throughout the company.

Given the complexity of the manager self-service system, it is generally best to roll out only one function at a time, not only to ensure that sufficient system checking is conducted, but also to give managers sufficient time to train on each function and become used to its mode of operation.

Cost: 💸 💸 💸   *Installation time:* 🕰 🕰 🕰

8.21 Automate Employment and Income Verification Requests

The payroll department of larger companies can be buried by the large volume of employment and income verification requests that it receives from lenders and other third parties who need this information in order to complete various financial transactions with employees. Although generally only a hire date and current salary level are needed, the sheer volume of these requests can be burdensome, because each one requires accessing employee payroll records and also may require some phone tag with the requesting party.

A better approach is to automate the verification process, so that third parties are required to go to a Web site to access the information. A good example is *www.theworknumber.com*, which is run by the TALX company. Under this approach, employees access the Web site, locate their company name, and enter their social security and PIN numbers. The system asks them if they want to provide employment and/or salary information to a requesting party. If so, the Web site responds with a salary code, which the requesting party can use to access the required information over the Web site. To prevent abuse, the salary access privilege automatically expires, so the requesting party cannot continue to review the employee's pay information over a long period of time. The payroll manager also can access the system to review transaction volumes.

TALX estimates that this service is not cost effective unless a company has at least 3,500 employees, which puts it out of the range of most organizations. Nonetheless, a company determined to try this approach could design its own system using the same data accessibility technique, with the added advantage of having a direct data feed into the application, over which it would have complete control.

Cost: 💵 💵   Installation time: 🕙 🕙

Customer Service

8.22 Publish Answers to Frequently Asked Questions on an Intranet Site

Payroll departments spend a great deal of time answering employee questions about their pay. According to some surveys, this activity involves at least one-third of all department time. Although most of the questions are simple enough to answer, when they are multiplied by the number of employees in the company, it is easy to see how the payroll staff can spend so much time just responding to queries.

If the payroll staff could compile a list of the most commonly asked questions by employees, it would not be especially long—perhaps just 10 or 20 questions for a basic payroll system, and maybe twice that amount if the department also handles benefits through the payroll system. Given the high proportion of questions dealing with a limited number of issues, this is an ideal area in which to create answers to frequently asked questions (FAQs) and post them on a company intranet site. Employees then can be directed to the FAQs list and asked to address the payroll staff only regarding more complex questions. Sample FAQs follow.

Question: If I am on direct deposit, at what time of day on payday will my pay be deposited in my checking account?
Answer: Your pay will be available in your checking account as of 8 A.M. on payday.

Question: If payday falls on a weekend, when am I paid?
Answer: If the payday falls on a weekend, you will be paid as of the first business day prior to that weekend.

Question: Can I get an advance on my next paycheck?
Answer: No. The company policy is to never issue pay advances under any circumstances.

Question: If I resign from the company, when will I be paid my final paycheck?
Answer: If you voluntarily leave the company, you will be paid as part of the next regularly scheduled payroll.

Question: How much unused vacation time can I roll forward into next year?
Answer: You can roll 40 hours forward. For exceptional cases, you must apply to your department manager for a waiver.

Although these FAQs also can be listed in the employee manual, employees do not always refer to that document. By also presenting them on the intranet site (which employees tend to access more frequently, especially if it is a rich, multifunction site), there is a much greater chance that employees will access the FAQs instead of the payroll staff.

Cost: 🐖   *Installation time:* ⏰

8.23 Operate a Payroll Help Desk

In larger companies with many employees, servicing employee requests for information consumes a massive amount of time within the payroll department. As noted in the preceding best practice, these requests can consume up to one-third of all staff time, which can severely debilitate the department when trained payroll specialists are constantly being called away from their work to deal with employee issues.

A good alternative is to create a payroll help desk, staffed by people who specialize in answering employee payroll questions. Exceptionally large organizations may require the creation of a formal call center, armed with customer relationship management (CRM) software. There are a number of CRM software suppliers, such as Siebel, Microsoft, and Vantive. Software more specifically designed for help desks is produced by dozens of companies, including Applix, IssueTrak, and Avensoft. The software chosen should fit the company's needs for identifying and tracking employee issues, so the payroll manager is aware of multiple occurrences of the same inquiries; employee issues also must be addressed rapidly. It is extremely important that the payroll manager can easily determine the status of all open employee issues in order to achieve the highest possible level of employee satisfaction with the help desk. Whatever system is used, it is critical that the payroll staff members review messages from the help desk on a regular basis, so they can answer questions too detailed for the help desk staff to answer.

Companies with larger payroll help desk installations should consider combining forces with the human resources department, so the call center can answer questions on behalf of both departments. By doing so, the payroll department likely will incur a somewhat lower operating cost for the help desk, while employees will be able to access a single help desk for answers to a broader range of questions on more topics.

An alternative for companies spending large amounts of time managing call center operations is to outsource this function to a third party. Many companies specialize in this service and would be happy to take over the task. However, one must be sure to understand their fee structure, their hours of operation, required links into the company computer systems, and where the call center will be located; within the country where employees are located is better for this application, because employees need to talk to people with an excellent command of the language.

Cost: 💰 💰   *Installation time:* ⏱ ⏱

8.24 Implement a Service-Level Agreement with Other Departments

The payroll department is a cost center, where the payroll manager is responsible for incurring the smallest possible total cost. This cost is usually well defined through the annual budget. However, there is also a minimum level of service required of the department that is not defined at all. This service primarily includes the accumulation of time worked information, its translation into an accurate period payroll check for each employee, tax remittances to various governments, and mandatory payroll reporting. The trouble is that other department managers regularly ask for services in addition to this, such as off-cycle bonus checks, payroll advances, employee deductions for special purchases made through the company, demands for more frequent pay cycles, and so on. These extra services are expensive, and they are usually not addressed in the annual budget, so the payroll manager is placed in the uncomfortable position of battling with other department managers to keep from providing extra services that would otherwise result in the incurrence of excessive costs.

The solution is to create a service-level agreement (SLA). This document lists what the payroll manager and signatory department managers have mutually agreed to expect from the payroll department in terms of various services, thereby creating formal documentation of service levels that can be tied back to the budgeting process. Such documentation makes the allocation of resources within the payroll department much easier for the payroll manager.

The SLA can include provisions for not running off-cycle payrolls, or at least charging a fee for this service to the department asking for the service. It also can itemize the metrics under which the payroll department is to be measured and to which it commits to meet certain target levels. The key target to strive for when constructing an SLA is to focus tightly on just those performance standards that are of most importance to the other departments, rather than creating an ultra-detailed document that covers every aspect of the payroll department and how it functions; the intent is to create a governing document that addresses the few key issues that matter most to other departments, not something that looks like a detailed union labor agreement.

Cost: 🖋   *Installation time:* ⏰⏰

8.25 Designate Intermediaries to Maintain Contact with Fellow Service Providers

The payroll department is by no means the only service provider within a company, especially a larger organization. There is also the human resources department, possibly a separate staff devoted to employee relocations, stock benefits, retirement, and perhaps even a call center that handles employee queries. It is entirely possible that actions taken by one of these fellow service providers will have an impact on the payroll department. For example, if the employee relocation group decides to require employee payment for spouse travel to search for a new home, the payroll department may be asked to deduct these costs from employee pay.

A simple way to coordinate the activities of the various service providers, or at least to keep the payroll manager abreast of developments in these other areas, is to designate a payroll employee as an intermediary with each one. Doing this may result is a monthly visit to chat or perhaps a more formal documented meeting, with minutes being sent to the various department managers. If there is a great deal of interaction between departments, it may even be necessary to create SLAs to document what services each department will provide. If so, these SLAs can be administered or monitored by the designated intermediaries.

Cost: 🖋   *Installation time:* ⏰⏰

Miscellaneous Topics

8.26 Use the Common Paymaster Rule to Reduce Payroll Taxes

When a company has multiple subsidiaries, it is possible that it will pay more payroll taxes than is required by the law. This happens when employees transfer between subsidiaries during the calendar year; every time they switch, they begin compiling their social security wage base all over again with a different payroll department, so they never have a chance to reach the current maximum wage base. Because the company matches the social security payments to the government, the company pays additional payroll taxes if an employee would otherwise have exceeded the maximum wage base. The same concept applies to federal unemployment taxes (FUTA). Although employees can recover their share of these excess withholdings, employers are not allowed to do so.

A company organized as a corporation can take advantage of the Common Paymaster rule to avoid paying these extra taxes. Under this concept, a corporation can calculate payroll taxes for employees being paid by multiple subsidiaries as if they were being paid by a single organization for the entire year. These conditions must be met for the Common Paymaster rule to apply:

- The paying parties must be "related," where either (1) a single company owns at least one-half the stock of the other related companies, (2) at least 30% of the employees of one corporation must be concurrently employed by the other corporation, or (3) at least half of the officers of one corporation must be officers of the other corporation.

- If a company is a nonstock corporation, at least one-half the board of directors of one corporation must also serve on the board of the other corporation.

- All payments made to employees must be through a single legal entity; thus, the employee cannot be paid separately by multiple payroll departments within the same company.

The last condition is key—*all* payments must be made from a single entity. This calls for the consolidation of payroll departments in order to achieve the available savings under this best practice.

The same concept can be used when a company wishes to credit any wages paid to employees of a new acquiree to their wage base when being paid by the acquiring company. The Common Paymaster rule can be applied in this scenario if the acquirer has acquired substantially all of the assets of the acquiree and if the employees of the acquiree are immediately employed by the acquirer.

Cost: 💵   *Installation time:* 🕐

8.27 Review the Impact of Voluntary Unemployment Contributions

When a company lays off a significant number of employees, its unemployment tax is likely to rise in the following year. The tax rate increase is caused by the company paying out more in unemployment benefits than it paid to the government in unemployment taxes. States like to have companies maintain a reserve balance of paid-in unemployment taxes equating to 6 to 10% of their net taxable wages (known as a reserve ratio). The reserve ratio is applied to a tax rate table to determine what tax rate the company will be charged in the following year.

An option available in many states is to make a voluntary contribution in advance of the scheduled tax rate increase (as of this writing, states accepting voluntary contributions are Arizona, Arkansas, Colorado, Georgia, Indiana, Kansas, Kentucky, Louisiana, Massachusetts, Maine, Michigan, Minnesota, Missouri, Nebraska, New Jersey, New Mexico, New York, North Carolina, North Dakota, Ohio, Pennsylvania, South Dakota, Texas, Washington, West Virginia, and Wisconsin). Doing this can reduce the tax rate levied during the following year. If the amount of the contribution results in a rate reduction equivalent to more money than the contribution, then making a contribution is a cost-effective step to take. This sounds like an anomaly—why would the government allow a company to pay in less than it may take out in the form of unemployment benefits in the following year? The reason is that tax rates are based on a rate table that requires specific tax rates for a range of reserve ratios; if one's reserve ratio is close to the fringes of a range for which a specific tax rate applies, then it is possible that a slight increase in the existing reserve (i.e., the voluntary contribution) will bump the company into a different bracket in the table, where a lower tax rate applies. Thus, a contribution of just a few dollars could result in a lowered tax rate that saves a company several thousand dollars.

In those states where voluntary contributions are accepted, the annual notice for the next year's tax rate change will include a worksheet on which one can calculate the amount of contribution needed to impact the rate change by a specific fraction of a percent. Thus, the payroll manager will know exactly what impact the contribution will have on next year's tax rate before deciding to make a contribution. Be sure to verify these calculations before sending in a contribution payment, because payments are nonrefundable.

Cost: 🖰   *Installation time:* 🕑

8.28 Acquire the Unemployment Experience Rating of a Predecessor Organization

On occasion, a business organization must change its legal form of organization. For example, it may switch from a limited liability corporation to a "C" corporation in order to attract venture capital. When this happens, the newly created entity is assigned a default experience rating for unemployment tax purposes that is relatively high. If the company previously had built up a better experience rating through the accumulation of large reserves or through minimal layoffs, it is faced with the prospect of rebuilding its experience rating as well as a new unemployment reserve fund, which usually takes several years. During that time, it must pay a higher unemployment tax rate than would otherwise have been the case.

The solution is to apply for a transfer of the old entity's experience rating to the new entity. This solution is allowable when the successor entity has acquired essentially all of the business of the predecessor entity and continues that business. This solution also applies if one entity has acquired another entity. A third variation is if two entities have acquired portions of the original entity, in which case they can apply for a split of the original entity's experience rating, based on the proportion of taxable payroll being transferred to each acquiring entity. When a rating transfer occurs, the succeeding business acquires the predecessor's unemployment funds reserve, charges against that reserve, and contributions into the reserve.

In order to acquire an experience rating in this manner, most states have limited time lines following the change of business entity, during which time an application must be made. If the application is not made during this period, the successor entity loses its right to acquire the earlier experience rating. Application forms are available through the various state governments, typically through the secretary of state, the department of revenue, or the department of unemployment (names will vary by state).

Cost: 💵   *Installation time:* ⏰⏰

9

Payroll Systems

This chapter contains eight best practices related to the use of large-scale software systems to assist the payroll function. The best practices are ranked in declining order of importance through the first seven items, followed by a negative best practice (what *not* to do) at the end of the chapter. A summary of the payroll systems, including a ranking of their costs and installation time, is shown in Exhibit 9.1.

The most important best practice in this chapter involves the consolidation of disparate payroll systems into a single system. By doing so, a company can improve the efficiency of its payroll processing greatly, while also reducing staffing levels and centralizing the payroll database. Once that best practice has been achieved, using an integrated human resources (HR) and payroll system can bring about the same types of efficiencies by merging the efforts of the HR and payroll departments. Next in line is an

Exhibit 9.1   Payroll Systems Best Practices Summary

	Best Practice	Cost	Install Time
9.1	Consolidate payroll systems	💵💵💵	⏰⏰⏰
9.2	Install an integrated human resources and payroll system	💵💵💵	⏰⏰⏰
9.3	Install an enterprise workforce management system	💵💵💵	⏰⏰⏰
9.4	Install a work-flow management system	💵💵💵	⏰⏰
9.5	Implement document imaging	💵💵💵	⏰⏰⏰
9.6	Install a data warehouse	💵💵💵	⏰⏰⏰
9.7	Use a forms/rates data warehouse for automated tax filings	💵💵💵	⏰⏰⏰
9.8	Avoid legacy payroll systems	💵💵	⏰⏰⏰

enterprise workforce management system, which improves overall staffing utilization. A work-flow management system is also highly recommended for larger companies, because it yields greater control over the processing of larger numbers of distributed payroll transactions. The remaining systems are more specialized, only impacting lesser aspects of the payroll department.

All of the best practices noted in this chapter involve significant investments of both time and money, and so require considerably more management support and planning than is the case for other best practices in this book.

9.1 Consolidate Payroll Systems

A company that grows by acquisition is likely to have a number of payroll systems—one for each company it has acquired. This situation also may arise for highly decentralized organizations that allow each location to set up its own payroll system. Although this approach allows each location to process payroll in accordance with its own rules and payment periods, while also allowing for local maintenance of employee records, the consolidation of all these systems into a single, centralized payroll system can solve several serious problems.

One problem with multiple payroll systems is that employee payroll records cannot be shifted through a company when an employee is transferred to a new location. Instead, the employee is listed as having been terminated in the payroll system of the location he or she is leaving and then is listed as a new hire in the payroll system of the new location. By constantly reentering an employee as a new hire, it is impossible to track the dates and amounts of pay raises; the same problem arises for the HR staff, who cannot track eligibility dates for medical insurance or vesting periods for pension plans. In addition, every time employee data are reentered into a different payroll system, there is a risk of data inaccuracies that may result from such embarrassments as wrong pay rates or mailing checks to the wrong address. Also, a company cannot easily group data for company-wide payroll reporting purposes. Finally, the company as a whole must pay more matching social security and Medicare expenses for employees if they switch between payroll systems during the year (see best practice 8.26 about the Common Paymaster rule). For all these reasons, it is common practice to consolidate payroll systems into a single, centralized location that operates with a single payroll database.

Before embarking on such a consolidation, one must consider the costs of implementation. A consolidation of many payroll systems can require an expensive new software package that must run on a larger computer, which entails extra capital and software maintenance costs (although the reverse may be the case: Consolidating multiple large payroll systems may result in the *elimination* of multiple software maintenance fees, depending on the circumstances). In addition, there is probably a significant cost associated with converting the data from the disparate databases into the new consolidated one. Further, there may be extra time needed to test the tax rate for all company locations in order to avoid penalties for improper tax withholdings and submissions. Finally, the timing of the implementation is of some importance. Many companies prefer to make the conversion on the first day of the new year, so there is no need to enter detailed pay information into the system for the prior year in order to issue year-end payroll tax reports to the government. The cost of consolidating payroll systems is considerable and must be carefully analyzed before reaching the decision to convert.

Cost: 🟢🟢🟢   *Installation time:* ⏰⏰⏰

9.2 Install an Integrated Human Resources and Payroll System

The payroll department shares responsibility for a wide range of employee data with the HR department. The payroll staff stores data about employee start dates, addresses, deductions, and so on; the HR staff separately records the same information about the same employees. A common issue is for an employee to update this information with one department but not the other, resulting in inconsistent data. Also, a major employee event, such as marriage, may be recorded by the payroll department for tax withholding purposes, but is never communicated to the HR staff, which needs this information to alter employee benefit packages. Thus, continual manual reconciliations of employee data between the two departments are needed.

A high level of data integration can be achieved by replacing these localized systems with an integrated one that uses a single database to provide full functionality to both departments. Doing this will involve replacing either or both of the systems currently in use, which is a major data conversion effort. It also entails training costs and the incurrence of ongoing software maintenance fees. Consequently, one must conduct a detailed cost-benefit analysis prior to making this investment.

Combined systems for large companies are available through the enterprise resources planning systems of Oracle (*www.oracle.com*) and SAP (*www.sap.com*); a variety of combined systems are available for smaller companies through such suppliers as Great Plains Software (*www.microsoft.com*) and Best Software (*www.bestsoftware.com*). It is also possible to obtain this level of fully integrated software solution through an outsourcing service. An example is Unicorn HRO (*www.unicornhro.com*). The system covers all aspects of human resources and payroll, including payroll processing, tax filings, benefits, 401(k), and COBRA administration.

A potential side effect of installing this combined system is that management may make the decision to merge the HR and payroll departments, on the grounds that a single manager will now be responsible for operation of the new system. If so, it is better to make this decision prior to the system installation, so the single manager can drive the overall implementation process as well as ongoing operation of the system.

Cost: 💵 💵 💵   *Installation time:* 🕑 🕑 🕑

9.3 Install an Enterprise Workforce Management System

When it comes to employees, the payroll department is concerned primarily with the collection of data about their time worked, which is then rolled into payroll calculations. However, other aspects of the timekeeping function are much more comprehensive and can be of considerable use to the company as a whole in using its employees in the most effective manner possible, resulting in greater profitability. For example, more advanced systems match employees to specific jobs based on their skills, certification levels, union rules, and other scheduling requirements. Many systems also allow employees to access their work schedules and trade shifts, as well as bid for more favorable schedules, resulting in higher employee morale. They can also warn of any number of violations, such as excessive overtime taken, a breach of union work rules, and excessive labor usage in comparison to a budget. Examples of suppliers that provide this software are ADI (*www.aditime.com*), ADP (*www.adp.com*), Ceridian (*www.ceridian.com*), Cignify (*www.cignify.com*), InfoTronics (*www.infotronics.com*), Kronos (*www.kronos.com*), SmartTime Software (*www.smarttime.com*), and Workbrain (*www.workbrain.com*).

These systems are designed for large organizations with large staffs and are expensive to acquire and maintain. Nonetheless, they can be a boon for those companies where strict attention to staffing utilization is a key driver of profitability.

Cost: 💵 💵 💵   *Installation time:* 🕑 🕑 🕑

9.4 Install a Work-Flow Management System

A number of transactions within the payroll department require approvals of various kinds or interaction with employees. In either case, it is likely that a transaction will be put on hold until some critical piece of paperwork is signed and returned to the payroll department. Depending on how responsive employees are in completing their parts of these transactions, the payroll department may find itself waiting a long time before it can complete the transactions.

The nature of many payroll transactions makes them an ideal candidate for a work-flow management system (WMS). A WMS is used to allocate work among large numbers of employees handling very large transaction volumes, with work being issued automatically to those employees most capable of handling it while ensuring that wait times are minimized. Although the work allocation functionality is not needed for payroll transactions, the other features of a WMS are useful.

There are four advantages to using a WMS:

1. Because it routes work to employees in a specific order, it can be designed to enforce the use of very specific payroll procedures. This can be a considerable benefit if the payroll staff is inexperienced or prone to making procedural mistakes. It is also useful if the payroll manager is constantly tweaking procedures on an ongoing basis, and wants the system to reflect the latest changes.

2. A work-flow product records processing history, including who was assigned a task, how long the task took to complete, and the results of this action—all excellent information for a postmortem review of each payroll transaction. This history yields accurate information about process and wait time durations that can be used to constantly refine processes.

3. The payroll manager can monitor the progress of each transaction in real time through the system to see who is handling each step at any given moment. If there are many people using the system in distributed locations, this can be an excellent way to manage the flow of payroll transactions.

4. The system usually can track which employees are away on vacation, training classes, and so on, and can route work tasks to other backup staff automatically to ensure that transactions are not delayed.

In order to make a work-flow management product an effective part of the payroll department, it is useful to create interfaces to the underlying payroll and HR systems, so an employee can click on a task and have the work-flow system automatically launch the required program and access the specific document called for by the payroll step. Also, if payroll tasks are being completed throughout a multidivision company, the work-flow product must be accessible from all these locations, which calls for real-time links to a central work-flow database.

A few examples of how a WMS can improve payroll functions are:

- *Personal updates.* Periodically issue a mass notification to all employees to verify their address, emergency contact, and other payroll and HR information, with links directly into the payroll database, so they can make these changes themselves.

- *W-4 updates.* In accordance with federal law, notify all employees at least once a year to review their W-4 statements, including a link to a W 4 form and a means to forward an electronic copy to the payroll department.

- *Benefits updates.* When benefits change, issue a mass notification to all employees to review their existing benefit package and make changes as needed. Because this is time critical due to benefit sign-up dates, the WMS is especially effective for determining which employees have not yet updated this information.

- *Employee handbook updates.* Periodically issue updates to the employee manual and have employees verify online that they have read it.
- *Process pay changes.* Managers can use a WMS to fill out pay change forms online, attach employee review forms, and forward the forms to a supervisor for approval. This process may pass through several approvals before being routed to the payroll department for processing.

The *www.waria.com* Web site offers an overview of many work-flow management suppliers. The site contains a supplier database, product descriptions, industry news, a bookstore, and a list of events. It is maintained by the Workflow and Reengineering International Association. Other sites providing similar information about work flow are *www.e-workflow.org*, *www.bpmi.org*, and *www.aiim.org*.

Cost: 💵 💵 💵   Installation time: 🕐 🕐

9.5 Implement Document Imaging

Many payroll departments constantly must search for files. Perhaps both the payroll and the HR departments need the same file, so the documents are constantly being borrowed from storage, resulting in no one being able to locate them consistently. Also, some employees are better than others at returning files when they are finished with them, and other companies just have a hard time obtaining a qualified group of people who can file documents in the right place. Whatever the case may be, it is a common problem and one that can seriously impact payroll operations.

An answer to this quandary is to convert all paper documents into digital ones and store them in the central computer system so that, potentially, all employees can access them from all locations—and do so at the same time. Digital documents have the advantage of never being lost (unless improperly indexed, as noted later in this section), never being destroyed (as long as there are proper backup routines), and being available to anyone with the correct kind of access. These are formidable advantages and have caused many larger corporations to adopt this approach as the best way to avoid the majority of their filing problems.

To implement a document imaging system, one must first obtain a document scanner with a sufficiently high throughput speed and resolution to allow scanning a multitude of documents, as well as scanning with a sufficient degree of clarity to obtain a quality digital image. This scanner must be linked to a high-capacity storage device, usually one containing multiple compact discs that is called a CD jukebox, and a file server containing the index file that tracks the location of all digital documents stored in the jukebox. A number of terminals are also necessary to link to this system, so that users may access digitized documents from as many computer locations as necessary. A graphical view of this layout is shown in Exhibit 9.2.

Some problems with digital document storage make it useful only in selected cases. One is cost: The entire system, especially the storage device, can easily bring the total cost into the six-digit range, with high-end systems for large corporations exceeding $1 million. Also, setting up the system entails a considerable workload, for a large portion of the department's existing documents, as well as new documents that are generated each day, must be scanned into the system. In addition, if a document is not properly indexed when it is first scanned into the system (i.e., given

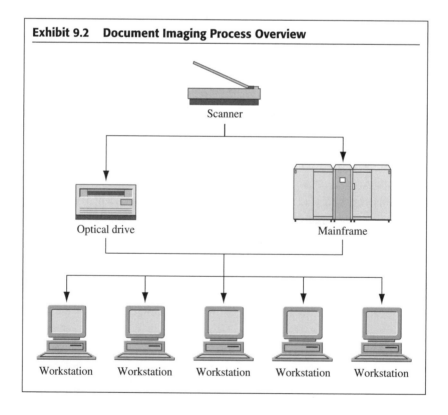

Exhibit 9.2   Document Imaging Process Overview

Scanner

Optical drive   Mainframe

Workstation   Workstation   Workstation   Workstation   Workstation an access code that allows a user to find it more easily), it is possible that there will be great difficulty in later locating it in the computer; in effect, the document is lost in the storage device. Thus, there are a number of issues to be aware of before installing such a system. Generally speaking, the cost consideration alone will keep smaller companies from implementing this solution.

Cost: 💵 💵 💵   *Installation time:* 🕰 🕰 🕰

9.6 Install a Data Warehouse

If a company outsources its payroll processing function, the underlying data will reside off-site and are not readily accessible except in the form of any standard or custom reports that the company has the payroll supplier print. The same lack of data arises for a company with multiple payroll systems, because each uses a separate payroll database that is not consolidated easily. The problem can occur even in a single-location, in-house payroll system if the underlying payroll processing software does not include an ad hoc querying capability. This lack of reporting capability is a significant problem, because the wage expense can be the largest company expense, and yet management has little insight into its details.

A possible solution is to create a data warehouse. This is essentially a single central database with an excellent reporting and ad hoc query software package attached to it. The data stored in this warehouse are extracted from the divisional payroll systems using either automated or manually triggered interfaces and are cleaned with automated error-checking routines. The querying portion of the data warehouse is enabled through a separate online analytical processing (OLAP) tool sold by a number of suppliers, such as SAS (*www.sas.com*), Oracle (*www.oracle.com*), and IBM (*www.ibm.com*). An OLAP tool is intended to provide fast query responses, cope with a broad range of logic questions, and make available a wide range of potential reporting formats.

A properly installed OLAP is useful for a variety of payroll functions. For example, it can search through payroll transactions for anomalies and bring them to the attention of the payroll staff, which then uses the data warehouse to drill down through the flagged transactions to see what is wrong, correcting problems faster than would otherwise be the case. Also, management can formulate its own queries to find answers to very specific questions that cannot be ascertained through a standardized set of payroll reports.

Once implemented, the payroll staff can rely on the data warehouse as its central information source, rather than divisional payroll systems. The data warehouse also can be used as the central corporate report generator, which many users can access for a variety of payroll reports. Further, it can store data for longer periods than might be practical for the underlying payroll systems. Finally, a data warehouse allows access to users without giving them the ability to alter actual transactions, the primary versions of which are still stored elsewhere at the division level.

However, installing a data warehouse is a major undertaking, involving detailed analysis of data models throughout a company to ensure that the correct transactions are pulled from divisional payroll databases and forwarded to the central data repository. It requires numerous custom interfaces, as well as a high degree of ongoing maintenance to ensure that the interfaces still work and that the correct data are being centralized. If data are being stored off-site at a payroll supplier location, then the payroll manager also must pay for a customized data feed from the supplier site back to the data warehouse. Also, because the underlying mishmash of payroll systems has not been altered, there is still a high risk that divisional transaction error rates will be unacceptably high. Further, if divisional payroll staffs are allowed to alter their charts of accounts, the system interfaces must be revised constantly to map these changes into the proper accounts in the data warehouse. Finally, the volume of data stored in a data warehouse calls for an industrial-strength database at its core, such as IBM's DB2, which is an expensive purchase.

For more information about data warehousing, access *www.dw-institute .com*, which is operated by the Data Warehousing Institute.

Cost: 💵 💵 💵   Installation time: 🕐 🕐 🕐

9.7 Use a Forms/Rates Data Warehouse for Automated Tax Filings

Any organization that operates in a number of states will find that an inordinate number of payroll tax returns must be filed. The traditional way to meet these filing requirements is to keep a staff of tax preparation personnel on hand or to outsource some or all of these chores to a supplier. Either approach represents a significant cost. An alternative worth exploring is to store tax rates and forms in a database that can be used to prepare tax returns automatically in conjunction with other accounting information that is stored in either a general ledger or a data warehouse.

To make this best practice operational, there must first be a common database containing all of the information that normally would be included on a payroll tax return. This may call for some restructuring of the chart of accounts, as well as the centralization of company-wide data into a data warehouse (see best practice 9.6). Doing this is no small task, because the information needed by each state may vary slightly from the requirements of other states, calling for subtle changes in the storage of data throughout the company that will yield the appropriate information for reporting purposes.

The next step is to obtain tax rate information and store it in a central database. This information can be located manually by accessing the tax agency Web sites of all 50 states. This information then can be stored in the forms/rates data warehouse. An additional step is to create a separate program for each of the tax reports, so that a computer report is issued that mimics the reporting format used by each state. Then the information can be transferred manually from the computer report to a printout of the Portable Document File (PDF) of each state's tax form. Those programming staffs with a large amount of available time also can create a report format that exactly mirrors each state tax form, and which can be printed out, with all tax information enclosed within it, and immediately mailed out.

The trouble with this best practice is the exceptionally high programming cost associated with obtaining a complete automated solution. There are so many tax forms to be converted to a digital format that the development task is considerable. Accordingly, it is more cost effective to determine those tax forms that share approximately the same information and to develop an automated solution for them first. Any remaining tax forms that would require special programming to automate should be reviewed on a case-by-case basis to determine if it is cost-beneficial to complete further programming work or to leave a few stray reports for the tax preparation staff to complete by hand.

This best practice is most useful where there is a legacy payroll system in place (see best practice 9.8), where employees work in many states, and where the company is large enough to support the cost of such a large systems development project. This best practice can be avoided entirely through the use of payroll outsourcing, because suppliers issue tax reports to all state governments as part of their core payroll processing service.

Cost: 💵 💵 💵   *Installation time:* 🕐 🕐 🕐

9.8 Avoid Legacy Payroll Systems

Larger companies have developed their own payroll software over time and have arrived at a sort of nirvana, where their in-house systems are tailored precisely to their specific needs. Legacy systems are especially useful where there are complex work rule environments with associated complex pay structures, as are commonly found in union shops. However, legacy systems are difficult to maintain, requiring specialized programmer skills. They are also sometimes poorly documented, which requires even more staff with deep system knowledge to understand how they operate and how they can be altered. The net result is usually a high-cost payroll system, despite its close fit with a company's payroll needs.

A better solution is to migrate away from a legacy system and instead use one of several alternatives—outsourcing, an application service provider, or a commercial off-the-shelf system. Although these supplier-provided systems will rarely fit a company's specific needs as well as a legacy system, their total cost to operate is nearly always less than that of a legacy system. They also require minimal development staffing to operate and are updated regularly by their suppliers. The annual maintenance cost or processing fees associated with these alternatives may seem expensive, but when compared to the total cost of a legacy system, they are less expensive.

Cost: 💵 💵   *Installation time:* 🕐 🕐 🕐

10

Payroll Controls

This chapter contains 14 best practices related to controls over the payroll function. The chapter begins with the most basic control, involving data backups, and then proceeds through two physical security controls, to five preventive controls, and then finishes with a series of detective controls. Preventive controls are more useful than detective controls, because they are designed to keep problems from occurring, whereas detective controls are designed to spot problems after they have occurred. Nonetheless, detective controls still play an important role in the payroll department, because one can use them to locate problems and make changes to the payroll system to ensure that they do not happen again. A summary of the controls, including a ranking of their costs and installation time, is shown in Exhibit 10.1.

Virtually all of the controls noted in Exhibit 10.1 are low cost and relatively easy to install. The only exception is the final best practice, which is a review of ineligible family members, because this task sometimes is assigned to a third party, which charges a fee for the service.

10.1 Create a Backup System for Payroll Records

Under the Fair Labor Standards Act (FLSA), employers are required to retain for two years a sufficient degree of payroll record detail to show how wage computations are based. This detail can include time cards and piecework tickets, wage rate tables, work and time schedules, and records of additions to or deductions from wages. If this information is not available and an employee brings suit about underpayment, a court can use the employee's records instead, however imperfect they may be, in deciding the case.

Exhibit 10.1 Payroll Controls Best Practices Summary

	Best Practice	Cost	Install Time
10.1	Create a backup system for payroll records	💵	🕐
10.2	Isolate access to the payroll check printing capability	💵	🕐
10.3	Scan fingerprints at user workstations	💵	🕐
10.4	Incorporate copy protection features into checks	💵	🕐
10.5	Implement positive pay	💵	🕐
10.6	Initiate direct deposit prenotifications	💵	🕐
10.7	Create standard error-checking reports	💵	🕐 🕐
10.8	Review payroll trends after each pay run	💵	🕐
10.9	Create standard payroll audit reports	💵	🕐 🕐
10.10	Reconcile the payroll bank account every day with online Internet access	💵	🕐
10.11	Verify that the payroll database has been updated with all manual checks	💵	🕐
10.12	Verify amounts owed by employees at termination	💵	🕐
10.13	Verify that year-end paid leave balances are properly accrued and carried forward properly	💵	🕐
10.14	Review insurance for presence of ineligible family members	💵 💵	🕐 🕐

To keep such a situation from arising, one can take a variety of actions. The simplest option is to collect all payroll records into marked storage boxes, indicating the number of years of retention, and store them in a secure location. At a more advanced level, one can digitize the same information, store it on a compact disc (CD), and keeping the CD in a fireproof safe, although the digitizing cost may be unacceptably high. A third variation is to keep all these records in electronic format from the start and adopt both on-site and off-site record storage polices that require multiple backup copies to be kept in multiple locations.

Cost: 💵   *Installation time:* 🕐

10.2 Isolate Access to the Payroll Check Printing Capability

Payroll is usually a company's largest expense, so the amount of funds retained in the payroll bank account can be considerable, in order to cover any checks issued against the account. This account represents an inviting target for anyone wanting to commit fraud by gaining access to the paycheck printing function.

To reduce the risk of fraud, one should limit access to the payroll check printing capability. There are several ways to do so. First, one should install the check-writing software on a specific computer, not on the company network; this forces a thief to gain physical access to a single computer, which can be heavily protected with access controls. Possible forms of access control include password protection that is changed at frequent intervals, biometric security access to the room where the computer is housed, and storage of paycheck blank stock in a locked cabinet. It is especially useful if the person having access to the check stock is different from the one having access to the check-writing software, so at least two people must be involved in any act of fraud. Also, from the perspective of a detection control, one should consider installing audit software that tracks who accessed the computer, when they did so, and exactly what commands they entered into the system.

Cost: 🖂 *Installation time:* 🕅

10.3 Scan Fingerprints at User Workstations

Security is always at issue in the payroll department, where the staff is constantly reviewing confidential information. It is a real problem trying to keep unauthorized personnel from accessing payroll terminals, unless the entire department is to be locked up behind a fence.

A unique new approach to solving the security problem is to use a variety of input devices that scan one's thumbprint or fingerprint and transmits the scan to a central file for verification. If the scanned image matches that of an on-file thumbprint, then the user is allowed access to the terminal.

A scanner mouse, called the Secugen OptiMouse™, is available from Secugen Corporation (*www.secugen.com*). The same company also sells a keyboard, called the Secugen KeyBoard™, that contains a scanner for fingerprints. Yet another option that it sells is called the Secugen Hamster™, which is a separate scanning device used by those who do not wish to replace their existing mice or keyboards.

There are a few downsides to the use of this technology. One is that some software reconfiguration will be necessary to ensure that selected databases are covered by this security feature. A lesser issue is the cost of the new scanning equipment; prices are roughly double the amount that one would spend on mice or keyboards that do not contain these biometric security features.

Cost: 🖎   Installation time: 🕰

10.4 Incorporate Copy Protection Features into Checks

Although the situation occurs rarely, occasionally check counterfeiters either modify a paycheck created by a company or create an entirely new one, resulting in significant losses to the company. A number of check protection features are available that can be incorporated into the company check stock in order to thwart the efforts of counterfeiters. Some of the features that can be ordered from the check printer are:

- *"Void" image.* When a check is copied, the word "Void" appears multiple times on the copied version of the check. This makes it impossible for a counterfeiter to create clean color copies of a check.
- *Microprinting border.* Text can be added along the edges of a check using very small fonts, so the words are visible as text only when magnified. When copied, they only appear as a line, with no discernible wording visible. This is a less obvious way to deter the efforts of someone attempting to color copy a check.
- *Modified background in dollar space.* A set of wavy lines can be built into the check in the area where the dollar amount is printed on the check. By doing so, counterfeiters will have a very difficult time erasing out existing dollar amounts without visibly damaging the background.

- *Watermark.* A watermark can be added to a check that is visible only when seen from an angle and that is impossible to duplicate when a check is run through a copier. This technique is most effective when the check contains a warning not to accept the check unless the watermark can be seen.

  Cost: 💰   *Installation time:* 🕐

10.5 Implement Positive Pay

Some payroll departments have a problem with check fraud, whereby checks are presented to the bank for payment that either were not issued by the company or were issued for a lesser amount than is noted on the presented checks. Although this problem is not normally a large one, some companies can lose a considerable amount of money to fraudulent activities by this means.

A few banks now allow companies to use a program called "positive pay," which virtually eliminates check fraud. This best practice works by having an organization send to the bank a daily list of all checks issued, which usually is stored in a specific data storage format that the bank can use to update its files of authorized checks that it is allowed to cash. All presented checks are compared to this master list, with both the check number and amount being reviewed. If there is a discrepancy, the check is rejected. By using this method, check fraud can be completely eliminated.

However, only a few larger banks offer this program. Also, banks usually charge for this service, a cost that is difficult to justify in light of the infrequency of check fraud. There is an additional cost to the company for storing check data on a tape and sending it to the bank (although this can also be performed with a secure e-mail or Internet transaction). Finally, a major problem is that the organization must ensure that *all* checks are included in the information that it sends to the bank, or else some checks may be rejected for payment—this can be a major problem if manual paychecks are not loaded promptly into the payroll database. For all these reasons, positive pay tends to be useful in a minority of situations.

Cost: 💰   *Installation time:* 🕐

10.6 Initiate Direct Deposit Prenotifications

There are a surprisingly large number of errors in the initial setup of a direct deposit transaction, usually because either the employee has incorrectly forwarded the wrong bank account routing information to the payroll department or this information has then been incorrectly transcribed into the direct deposit database. Whatever the reason, the result is a cancelled direct deposit. If the company outsources its payroll processing, the payroll supplier automatically will issue a regular check payment instead. However, if payroll is processed internally, the payroll staff must have a procedure in place to spot the cancellation and then issue a check payment instead. If the procedure is not in place, the result will be an extremely unhappy and unpaid employee. Even if the check is paid at the correct time, manual processing of the check may be required, which is very inefficient.

A good solution is always to require a prenotification transaction, which is essentially a test of the direct deposit account to ensure that the real payment will go through correctly at a later date. Prenotifications are standard practice for payroll suppliers, but this may not be the case if a company handles its own direct deposit transactions.

Cost: 🖦 *Installation time:* 🕐

10.7 Create Standard Error-Checking Reports

The payroll staff may deal with such a large volume of payroll transactions during each payroll cycle that it cannot comb through 100% of the entries to verify that the resulting paychecks will be perfect. As a result, it is common to have employees complain about incorrect pay, missing pay, or incorrect deductions. Given the criticality of these errors to employees, the payroll manager usually needs to run an off-cycle payroll to fix these problems.

A good solution is to write standard error-checking reports that are run as part of every payroll. These reports only show unusual transactions that fall outside the normal pay boundaries, and so are a good source of likely errors that can be investigated and corrected quickly. Examples of these reports are:

- *Active employees with no payments.* Indicates that timekeeping records may be missing.

- *Time entered for inactive employees.* Indicates that either an inactive employee has come back to work (which requires a variety of deduction activations), that an employee has charged time to the wrong employee code, or that some other employee is attempting to falsely record time on behalf of the inactive employee.

- *Leave balances are negative.* Indicates that an employee is taking more leave than is authorized. This calls for supervisory approval.

- *Negative deductions.* Indicates when a payment is being made to an employee via a negative deduction, requiring review for underlying causes.

- *Negative taxes.* Indicates either negative pay situations or cases where previous excess tax deductions are being corrected.

- *Hourly rate less than minimum wage.* Indicates that a payment is being made that is below the legal pay limit. This report may have to be sorted by state, because some state-mandated minimum wage rates are higher than others.

- *Hourly rate greater than $___.* This report is designed to catch very large hourly rates exceeding what any employee normally would receive.

- *Net pay greater than $___.* This report is designed to catch very large payments exceeding what any employee normally would receive.

These reports should be run by the payroll manager, because the issues they highlight could be indicative of fraudulent activity by the payroll clerk who enters transactions in the payroll system. Having the clerk run these reports would be similar to having the fox guard the henhouse.

Cost: 🖋️   *Installation time:* 🕐 🕐

10.8 Review Payroll Trends after Each Pay Run

The payroll department sometimes spots errors in a pay run well after it has been run and paychecks distributed. These problems, such as incorrect withholdings or deductions, frequently require adjustment prior to the next pay run, as well as a correcting entry to eliminate the impact of the original error. The department needs a way to increase its odds of spotting errors sooner, so it can complete a corrected pay run at once.

When external auditors review a company's accounting records at the end of each year, one of their principal tools for spotting problems is to compare the proportion of expenses in various expense categories to total revenues and then compare the resulting percentages to those incurred in the preceding few years. If any percentages are unusually high or low, they will focus considerable attention on determining why the changes have taken place. The payroll department can use the same approach. After every pay run, one can calculate the percentage of social security, Medicare, federal and state unemployment, and all other employee deductions as a percentage of the total wage and salaries expense. Then one can compare these percentages to the percentage calculations for all preceding pay runs for the past year. This approach may spot problems with mandatory deductions erroneously not being taken, large changes in withholding levels, people exceeding the maximum social security withholding level, and so on. For greater granularity in the data, one may consider running this calculation for individual departments within the company. It also may be possible to standardize this calculation with a custom report, so the calculation effort is minimized.

An added benefit of this approach is that the payroll manager can notify the accounting department of any reasons for unusual pay-related variances on a proactive basis, rather than waiting for an analyst from that department to ask the same questions at a later date. This rapid data feed to accounting assists the controller in closing the books somewhat faster each month, because he or she knows that payroll variances will be fully explained before the month closes.

Cost: 🖋️   *Installation time:* 🕰️

10.9 Create Standard Payroll Audit Reports

A larger company will have an internal audit department, and occasionally that department will schedule reviews of the payroll function. When it does, the audit team must deal with a considerable quantity of data, especially if there are over 1,000 employees with all their associated pay and timekeeping records. Auditing this much information expands the duration of the audit and requires the audit team to spend more time on data summarization and less on analysis, which is not a good use of its time.

Auditors are likely to review at least some of the same issues every time they audit the payroll department, so it is possible to set up standard audit reports for them in advance that will eliminate all data summarization tasks. Some possibilities for prepackaged audit reports are:

- *Annualized/hourly pay rates, sorted by employee.* Used to compare to signed pay change authorizations, to determine if employees are being paid the correct amounts.
- *Employee list, sorted by department.* Used to verify with department managers who currently is working for them, with the intent of determining if former or fake employees are being paid.
- *Full-year totals of hours worked, sorted by employee.* Used to ascertain if an employee should be categorized as a full-time or part-time employee, which is used to determine employee eligibility for the corporate benefits package.
- *Hours worked by specified day, sorted by employee.* Used to compare to any paper-based timekeeping documents to ensure that actual hours worked match those recorded in the payroll system.
- *List of employees with family insurance, sorted by employee.* Used to determine if employees have ineligible family members on their policies.
- *Summarization of overtime hours worked by employee, sorted in declining order by hours worked.* Used for determining possible overtime abuse.

Cost: 🪙   *Installation time:* 🎲🎲

10.10 Reconcile the Payroll Bank Account Every Day with Online Internet Access

If the payroll staff needs to know the current balance outstanding on the payroll checking account balance, the most common way to find out is to call the company's bank representative. This approach is slow and sometimes inaccurate, because the bank representative may not be available or may misread the information appearing on the screen.

An easier approach is to access detailed account information through a Web site. This access is usually free, requires no special software besides an Internet browser, and can be accessed at once, if the user is connected to a direct-access Internet connection, such as DSL, cable, or a T1 line. The better Web sites are also heavily engineered to be easy to read, with online automated help text to walk the user through the screens. This is becoming such a powerful tool that users should consider switching their bank accounts to those financial institutions offering this service. This is an especially strong control point for the payroll department, because one can quickly spot all unrecorded transactions, banking errors, and bank fees and update the internal accounting database with this information. Of particular interest is the ability to monitor uncashed paychecks through this system; because paychecks rarely remain uncashed for long, such lingering items can be evidence of an incorrect payment made to someone who is no longer an employee or of an unclaimed check that requires additional action by the payroll staff to notify the employee to whom the check belongs.

Cost: 💵   *Installation time:*   🕰️

10.11 Verify That the Payroll Database Has Been Updated with All Manual Checks

Despite its best efforts, the payroll department will issue a large number of manual checks over the course of a year. These checks are needed to handle smaller one-time payments that are not worth processing through an off-cycle payroll. The trouble is that someone must remember to enter the check manually in the payroll database, so the recipient's income and deductions are accurately portrayed on the year-end W-2 form. If not, employees will need a corrected W-2c form, and usually in a hurry in order to file income tax returns in a timely manner. Researching the reasons for the W-2c and issuing it take even more time. Consequently, it is extremely important that the payroll database be updated at once when manual checks are issued.

There are several ways to do so. One approach is to conduct a daily reconciliation of the payroll bank account, which can be done easily if there is

Internet access to the bank's daily records. Any unrecorded checks will become apparent through this reconciliation as soon as employees deposit the checks. However, this action will not spot checks that have been erroneously posted to an employee expense account through the accounts payable system. To spot this type of error, one should periodically run a report that is filtered to show only payments made to employees, and see if the check numbers on the report come from check associated with the payroll bank account, rather than the numeric sequence for checks drawn on the payables bank account. Of course, the check numbers for these two accounts must vary considerably from each other in order to make account posting errors apparent. The least effective approach is to review manually the employee and payables files to see if any manual checks have been filed there but not been posted to the payroll database.

Cost: 🪙   *Installation time:* ⏰

10.12   Verify Amounts Owed by Employees at Termination

There are a number of ways in which an employee can owe a company money, such as travel advances, pay advances, and purchases made through the company. There are also cases where employees are liable for the cost of training classes if they leave the company within a certain period of time following the training class. It is not uncommon for an employee to be terminated, with the payroll staff learning of these issues only after the fact. Usually there is no way to obtain payment from former employees, so the remaining balances must be written off.

The best way to ensure that employees pay for any owed amounts at the point of termination is to maintain a checklist of potential repayment items. Because there should already be a master termination checklist for other termination activities, such as returning company keys and issuing COBRA documents, it should be a simple matter to add these issues to the list. A sample termination checklist pertaining to these issues follows:

    ☐   Are all payroll advances repaid?
    ☐   Are all travel advances repaid?
    ☐   Are there any unpaid petty cash IOU vouchers?

☐ Are there any unpaid purchases through the company?

☐ Has the employee taken any classes in the past year requiring reimbursement?

Cost: 💸   *Installation time:* ⏰

10.13   Verify That Year-End Paid Leave Balances Are Accrued and Carried Forward Properly

The accrued vacation expense can be a significant expense in those companies that allow a great deal of vacation time to be carried forward. In cases where either a "use it or lose it" or a maximum carry-forward policy is in place, it is possible that employees will lose a significant amount of their accrued vacation time at year-end, which impacts not only the employees but also the size of the vacation accrual. If the accrual is not adjusted correctly for the impact of this year-end policy, the external auditors may make a substantial adjusting entry as part of their year-end audit that will not please the corporate controller. In addition, the internal vacation tracking system must roll forward any allowed vacation balances properly, so the balances are accessible by employees in the following year.

One part of the solution is to monitor closely the vacation accrual on an employee-by-employee basis over the course of the year, accruing a vacation expense equivalent to the expected year-end balance. One must adjust this accrual for any changes in pay rates, used vacation time, accrued vacation time, and supervisor-approved overrides to the year-end carry-forward policy. Given the potential complexity of this accrual, it may make sense to have a formal procedure for completing it each month. For smaller companies, a simple spreadsheet is an adequate tool for conducting this review. In larger companies with many employees, it is better to automate as much of the process as possible by linking data from the timekeeping system and pay rate file to create a standard vacation accrual report.

As soon as possible after year-end, the payroll staff also should verify on a spot-check basis that employee vacation balances have been rolled forward into the next year correctly. This review cannot wait, because employees are likely to spot (and complain about) errors very early in the new year.

Cost: 💸   *Installation time:* ⏰

10.14 Review Insurance for Presence of Ineligible Family Members

The cost of health insurance for family members can exceed three times the cost of the same insurance for single employees. Because of this, health insurance is frequently the second-largest expense that a company must manage. The focus of this cost management tends to be on the type of health plans offered to employees or the size of the deductible. However, a considerable hidden cost is the presence of family members on the health plans who are no longer eligible to receive benefits, such as overage children or ex-spouses. Payroll departments in smaller companies may be responsible for the health care plan, and so need to find ways to reduce this expense.

There are several ways to reduce health costs by removing ineligible dependents from the corporate health care plan. The minimal approach is to have employees update dependent information as part of the annual benefits renewal process, but employees may have a significant monetary incentive to continue claiming dependents; otherwise they will have to pay for the expense themselves. A slight improvement is to conduct random spot checks of employees and make sure that these checks are publicized. By doing so, all employees are aware that they may have to pay back unearned benefits. A more intensive approach is to conduct a thorough periodic audit to verify the eligibility of dependents, which can include a first phase that allows employees to change the status of their dependents without penalty. Because a full audit is expensive, a reasonable middle-of-the-road approach is first to conduct spot checks to see if there is a problem and then to expand to a full audit if the initial results indicate the need to do so.

Cost: 💵 💵   *Installation time:* 🕐 🕐

11

Payroll Measurements

After having implemented any of the best practices noted in the previous chapters, one should determine the extent of any resulting changes. This chapter contains seven measurements related to inventory that can be used selectively to track the performance of the payroll staff, the cost of the function, and a variety of employee costs.[*] One should not feel compelled to use all seven measurements. Instead, one should use only those measurements needed to track the most important areas of emphasis within the department. Too many measurements constitute an overflow of information, and certainly require an excessive amount of effort to calculate. The measurements discussed are shown in Exhibit 11.1.

11.1 Payroll Transaction Fees per Employee

A great many companies have found that it is well worth the effort of outsourcing their payroll processing functions to specialized service providers,

---

Exhibit 11.1   Payroll Measurements Summary
11.1   Payroll transaction fees per employee
11.2   Payroll transaction error rate
11.3   Ratio of W-2c to W-2 forms issued
11.4   Proportion of payroll entries to headcount
11.5   Annualized wages per employee
11.6   Net benefits cost per employee
11.7   Revenue per employee

---

[*]Selected measurements in this chapter are used with permission from Steven M. Bragg, *Accounting for Payroll* (Hoboken, NJ: John Wiley & Sons, 2004), Chapter 5.

thereby eliminating the hassle associated with payroll tax calculations and submissions. However, few companies go to the trouble of determining the annual cost of this processing on a per-person basis. They may be startled to find that the initial cost at which they agreed to the service has ballooned over time, because of extra fees tacked onto the base processing rate for such services as direct deposit, sealing checks in envelopes, calculating special deductions, and tracking garnishments. For these companies, the payroll transaction fee per employee measurement is a valuable tool.

To calculate this measurement, divide the total payroll outsourcing fee by the total number of employees itemized on the payroll. Be sure to exclude from the total fee any charges that cannot be directly related to individual employees, such as special reports or payroll shipping charges. The formula is:

$$\frac{\text{Total payroll outsourcing fee per payroll}}{\text{Total number of employees itemized in payroll}}$$

As an example, a new payroll manager has been hired at the Jebson Maintenance Company, which has a large staff of heating and ventilation maintenance technicians. Accordingly, the payroll function is the key accounting activity. The new manager is interested in obtaining the best cost-benefit performance from the payroll function, which currently is outsourced. The manager compares the cost of the current outsourcing provider and the fees charged by a competitor (see Exhibit 11.2), which are all based on the processing of a single biweekly payroll:

Exhibit 11.2   Competing Payroll Supplier Fee Schedules

Types of Fees	Current Provider Fees	Competitor Fees
Minimum processing fee	$50	$15
Processing fee/each	$1.00	$1.25
Envelope stuffing fee/each	$.15	$.25
Delivery fee	$10	Free
Direct deposit fee/each	$.50	$.65
401(k) report	$12	$5
Sick time report	$10	$5
Garnishment fee/person	$2.50	$3.50

The company has 26 payrolls per year and 120 employees, all of whom take direct deposit payments. The company has requested 401(k) and sick time reports once a month. There are 10 employees whose wages are garnished. Based on these volume considerations, the total cost of the current provider is:

Variable cost per year = Processing fee of $1.00 × 120 employees × 26 payrolls
                          = Envelope stuffing fee of $.15 × 120 employees × 26 payrolls
                          = Direct deposit fee of $.50 × 120 employees × 26 payrolls
                          = Garnishment fee of $2.50 × 10 employees × 26 payrolls
                          = $5,148

Fixed cost per year = Minimum processing fee of $50 × 26 payrolls
                       = Delivery fee of $10 × 26 payrolls
                       = 401k report charge of $12 × 12 months
                       = Sick time report charge of $10 × 12 months
                       = $1,824

Total cost per year = $6,972

Using the same methodology, the total cost of the competitor's offer is:

Variable cost per year = Processing fee of $1.25 × 120 employees × 26 payrolls
                          = Envelope stuffing fee of $.25 × 120 employees × 26 payrolls
                          = Direct deposit fee of $.65 × 120 employees × 26 payrolls
                          = Garnishment fee of $3.50 × 10 employees × 26 payrolls
                          = $7,618

Fixed cost per year = Minimum processing fee of $15 × 26 payrolls
                       = Delivery fee of $0 × 26 payrolls
                       = 401k report charge of $5 × 12 months
                       = Sick time report charge of $5 × 12 months
                       = $ 510

Total cost per year = $8,128

This analysis shows that the competitor's bid is $1,156 higher than that of the existing service provider, primarily because the competitor charges higher per-employee fees (despite having lower fixed service costs). In this case, the variable payroll cost per employee is $42.90 if the current supplier is used and $63.48 if the competitor is used.

As noted, one must segregate those charges that have nothing to do with the per-person fees associated with the payroll; in the example, these fees would be the minimum processing fee, delivery charge, and the two reports. By separating these costs, one can determine more easily the pricing strategies of payroll suppliers, some of whom advertise low fixed fees to attract new customers but have so many extra per-employee fees that the total cost is higher.

11.2 Payroll Transaction Error Rate

A great deal of data is brought together into the payroll processing function, especially if a company employs a large number of hourly personnel whose pay fluctuates from period to period. If there is an error in the payroll calculations, it generally requires an inordinate amount of time to recalculate pay and issue manual checks that address the problem. Consequently, it is useful to measure the payroll transaction error rate on a trend line in order to tightly control the number of errors generated.

To calculate the payroll transaction error rate, divide the total number of payroll errors for a payroll by the total number of payroll changes made during that payroll. Payroll changes may include changes to addresses, deductions, pay rates, exemptions, or married status. The denominator should *not* be the total number of employees listed in the payroll, since many of them may be salaried (which requires no payroll change), and so do not provide a true picture of the total number of transactional changes made to the payroll. The measurement is:

$$\frac{\text{Number of payroll transaction errors}}{\text{Total number of payroll entries}}$$

For example, the First Alert Company employs a large part-time staff that assembles thousands of first aid kits by hand. Its payroll staff is overwhelmed by the varying number of employees and changing hours to be

Exhibit 11.3   Error Totals by Payroll Transaction Type

Transaction Type	Total Number	Number of Errors
Address entry	9	1
Deductions entry	8	0
Employee addition/deletion	42	7
Exemptions entry	15	0
Hours entry	312	49
Status entry	3	0
Totals	389	57

charged, resulting in a constant stream of payroll adjustments. The controller, who wants to determine the payroll transaction error rate before spending a great deal of money to have a consultant review the payroll process and suggest ways to streamline it, assembles the information in Exhibit 11.3 from the last payroll.

Based on this information, the transaction error rate is 57/389, or 15%. More important, a review of the exhibit quickly reveals that the source of nearly all errors is the timekeeping system, which produced 49 errors in the number of hours entered into the system. The controller should focus the consultant's efforts in this area.

This measurement can be misleading when the payroll function is outsourced and a company employee is calling the information in to the payroll supplier, whose data entry clerk is entering the information into a payroll system. In this instance, it is difficult to tell if payroll errors originate with the person calling in the information or the data-entry clerk who is inputting it.

11.3 Ratio of W-2c to W-2 Forms Issued

If significant errors in the payroll process go undetected until year-end, they are likely to result in inaccurate W-2 forms being issued to employees. If so, the payroll department must reissue a corrected W-2 form, which requires a W-2c form. Because the effort required to correct a W-2 form can be considerable, it is useful to know what proportion of W-2c forms are issued in proportion to the total number of W-2 forms issued. Also, that proportion is a good general indicator of the level of accuracy of the underlying payroll transactions.

To calculate the ratio of W-2c to W-2 forms issued, one divides the total number of W-2c forms issued by the total number of W-2 forms issued. The measurement is:

$$\frac{\text{Total number of W-2c forms issued}}{\text{Total number of W-2 forms issued}}$$

For example, the Dolphin Aquatic company issues W-2 forms to all of its 529 employees, only to have 48 employees complain that their last paycheck totals were not included in their W-2 forms. After issuing revised W-2c forms, the company finds that its calculated error rate is 9% (derived from 48 W-2c forms/529 W-2 forms).

The only problem with this measurement is that W-2c forms may not be issued for quite a long time after W-2 forms are issued, because payroll errors may not come to light for some time. It is possible that some errors may be found several years later, as the result of tax audits. Thus, it is best to calculate the measurement at least a few months after the W-2 forms are issued initially and again the following year, if comparative measurements are maintained for previous years.

11.4 Proportion of Payroll Entries to Headcount

A payroll manager may be tracking too much information about employees through the payroll system; doing so requires an excessive number of payroll entries to maintain, leading to reduced efficiency. For example, the payroll staff may be required to make separate deductions for short-term disability insurance, long-term disability insurance, medical insurance, the cafeteria plan, dental insurance, health club charges, meals from the company cafeteria, and so on. By compiling the total number of payroll entries in the system per employee, one can see if this "data load" is excessive. If so, one can appeal to company management to eliminate some deductions entirely, or see if some deductions can be combined (i.e., a single deduction for all types of insurance), thereby reducing the payroll staff's workload.

The formula is to accumulate the number of all payroll deductions, memo entries, and goal entries and divide this total by the number of full-time equivalents. The formula is:

$$\frac{\text{Total deductions} + \text{Total memo entries} + \text{Total goal entries}}{\text{Total number of full-time equivalents}}$$

The payroll manager of the Crawly Worm Company, purveyor of fine garden worms for fishermen, likes to know everything about her employees and over time has built up a massive amount of line items in the payroll database to do this. Upon her retirement, the incoming manager decides to calculate the proportion of payroll entries to headcount to see if there is too much information being entered into the system. He accumulates the information shown in Exhibit 11.4.

There are 50 employees, so by dividing the total deductions of 319 by 50, the new manager arrives at a proportion of payroll entries to headcount of 6.4 per person.

This measurement can appear to show a small number of payroll entries per person even when there are a great many types of entries, because some of the entries will apply to only a few employees. As shown in the example, many types of insurance, such as short-term disability, will be taken by only a few employees, so the total number of payroll entries will appear to be relatively low. From the perspective of determining the proportion of entries for the payroll staff to make, this measurement still results in an accurate proportion, although one still may wish to reduce the overall number of payroll entry types.

Exhibit 11.4 Journal Entry Totals by Transaction Type

Information Type	Number of Entries
Medical insurance deduction	50
Dental insurance deduction	45
Long-term disability deduction	40
Short-term disability deduction	8
Cafeteria plan dependent deduction	12
Cafeteria plan medical deduction	10
Cafeteria plan dependent deduction goal	12
Cafeteria plan medical deduction goal	10
Vacation time remaining	50
Sick time remaining	50
Excess cost of life insurance memo entry	32
Total	319

11.5 Annualized Wages per Employee

A typical payroll register will show the hourly rate of pay and year-to-date pay accumulators for those members of the staff who are paid on an hourly basis. This information does not provide one with the total annualized rate of pay, which is useful when determining pay raises, comparing pay scales, or comparing in-house pay levels to industry or regional standards. The problem also arises for any employees who are paid on a commission basis or whose pay is a mix of fixed base pay and variable incentive pay. For these employees, maintaining an annualized wage calculation can be useful.

This calculation can be derived for either a single employee or a group, such as for everyone having the same job title. If the former, the calculation is simply to summarize all fixed base pay, wages, commissions, bonuses, overtime, and other variable pay. If the latter, then one summarizes the same calculation for all employees in the group and divides by the number of employees in the group. The calculation is:

$$\frac{\text{Fixed base pay} + \text{Wages} + \text{Commissions} + \text{Overtime} + \text{Bonuses} + \text{Total other variable pay}}{\text{Total number of full-time equivalents}}$$

For example, the payroll manager of the All Seasons Generating Company, a regional utility, is trying to determine the annualized wages per employee for the 12-person electrical engineering department. She obtains the information in Exhibit 11.5 for the department for the past 12 months.

The annualized wages per employee for this group are $742,000 divided by 12 employees, or $61,833. The manager notes that the overtime

Exhibit 11.5 Compensation Totals by Compensation Type	
Compensation Type	**Compensation Amount**
Total base pay	$ 0
Total wages	485,000
Total commissions	0
Total overtime	215,000
Total bonuses	42,000
Grand total	$742,000

compensation for this group is extremely high, which is caused by employees' being called out to repair damaged power transformers at all times of the day. The manager decides to recommend hiring more off-shift personnel in this area, which can reduce the amount of overtime paid and thereby reduce the total compensation cost in this area.

11.6 Net Benefits Cost per Employee

A company's managers make a number of small, incremental decisions related to employee benefits over time, frequently resulting in a wide array of benefits whose true cost is much higher than expected. Frequent use of this measurement tends to result in a much more conservative view of suggested additions to the existing benefits pool. Also, knowing the benefit cost per person allows one to decide whether it is less expensive to use contractors on a higher per-hour basis or to hire new employees at a lower hourly rate, but with benefits.

Benefit costs are best measured on a per-person basis, so the measurement should include all benefit costs in the numerator and the total number of full-time equivalent employees in the denominator. Benefit costs should include time taken off for vacations and sick time, all types of medical insurance (i.e., medical, dental, life, and disability insurance) net of employee deductions, and miscellaneous benefits, such as club memberships, dry cleaning costs, and company cars. The measurement is:

$$\frac{\text{Total cost of time off} + \text{Insurance} + \text{Other benefits} - \text{Employee deductions}}{\text{Total number of full-time equivalents}}$$

For example, the Sod Software Company, maker of operating systems for farmers, has assembled a high-powered group of 40 developers who have been attracted by the company and retained in large part by its excellent benefits package. Nonetheless, the company is finding that the package is extremely expensive, and must determine if any further additions to its staff will be of outside contractors who require no benefits. The payroll staff assembles the annualized benefits information shown in Exhibit 11.6.

By dividing the net total cost of $421,300 by the total headcount of 40 developers, the payroll staff finds that the net benefit cost per employee is $10,532.50.

Exhibit 11.6   Total Benefit Cost by Benefit Type

Benefit Type	Total Cost	Total Deductions	Net Total Cost
Medical insurance	$238,000	–$23,800	$214,200
Dental insurance	29,000	–2,900	26,100
Long-term disability	11,000	0	11,000
Short-term disability	27,000	0	27,000
Vacation time	80,000	0	80,000
Sick time	9,000	0	9,000
Company cars	40,000	0	40,000
Health club memberships	14,000	0	14,000
Totals	$448,000	–$26,700	$421,300

This measurement can be modified to show benefits as a percentage of total base pay. To continue the last example, if the average developer earned $75,000, then the total base pay would be $3 million, which would yield a benefits percentage of 14%. This percentage then could be tracked over time to spot changes or compared to industry standards to see if a company's benefit costs vary from the norm.

11.7 Revenue per Employee

Revenue per employee is one of the most closely watched of all performance measures. It is based on the assumption that employees are at the core of a company's profitability, and so high degrees of efficiency in this area are bound to result in strong profitability. It is also a standard benchmark in many industries.

To calculate this measurement, divide revenue for a full year by the total number of full-time equivalents (FTEs) in the company. An FTE is the combination of staffing that equals a 40-hour week. For example, two half-time employees would be counted as one FTE. The formula is:

$$\frac{\text{Annualized revenue}}{\text{Total full-time equivalents}}$$

A variation on this ratio is to divide annual revenues only by those FTEs who can be categorized as direct labor. This variation measures the productivity of those personnel who are directly connected to the manufacture of a company's products or services. This measure should be used with care, as it is not always easy to determine which employees can be categorized as direct labor and which ones fall into the overhead category instead. The formula is:

$$\frac{\text{Annualized revenue}}{\text{Total direct labor full-time equivalents}}$$

For example, the operations manager of the Twirling Washing Machine Company wants to determine the sales per person for the company, for all staff and for just the direct labor personnel. The company has annual revenues of $4,200,000. Its headcount is shown in Exhibit 11.7.

In total, the company has 54 employees. However, if we assume that the part-time staff all work half time, then the eight part-time positions can be reduced to four FTEs, which decreases the total headcount to 50 personnel. Another issue is what constitutes direct labor personnel—the company has a group of clearly defined direct labor personnel as well as a materials handling support staff and two production supervisors. The company can use any combination of these groups for its sales per direct labor measurement, as long as it consistently applies the measurement over time. However, the technically correct approach is to include in the measure any positions that are required for the proper completion of production efforts, which would require the inclusion of all three categories of labor. If this approach were not used, the person doing the measuring might be tempted to inflate the measurement results artificially by shifting direct labor personnel into other labor categories that fall just outside the definition.

Exhibit 11.7 Headcount by Department

Department	Headcount
Direct labor department	22
Direct labor part-time staff	6
Production supervisors	2
Material handling department	4
Sales, general & administrative	10
Administrative part-time staff	2
Engineering department	8

The result of these measurements is overall sales per employee of $84,000 (which is $4,200,000 in revenues, divided by 50 employees) and sales per direct labor employee of $135,484 (which is $4,200,000 in revenues, divided by 31 employees). The 31-employee figure is derived by adding 22 direct labor personnel to the 3 FTEs represented by the 6 part-time direct labor personnel, plus the production supervisors and material handling staff.

This formula is subject to a high degree of variation, depending how personnel are counted. For example, shifting away from employees to an outsourced solution or to the in-house use of temporary employees can artificially reduce the number of FTEs, as can the use of overtime by a smaller number of employees. Also, comparing the number of FTEs to revenue has a less direct bearing on profitability than comparing revenues to the total of all salaries and wages expenses; for example, one company with a large headcount but low pay per person may be more profitable than a company having a lesser headcount but a much higher salary per person. Also, some capital-intensive industries have so few employees in relation to the sales volume generated that this measure has much less significance than other measures, such as sales to fixed assets.

12

Payroll Policies and Procedures

A company's policies and procedures will change considerably if it installs a reasonable proportion of the best practices noted earlier in this book. Examples of likely changes are noted in the four sections of this chapter. The first section lists specific payroll policies designed to support a number of best practices. The next three sections address the three primary procedures used in the payroll department: timekeeping, payroll processing, and payment distribution. Each section includes a flowchart of the process flow before best practices are used, followed by a flowchart that incorporates best practices, and finishes with a formal procedure incorporating best practices improvements.

12.1 Policies for Payroll Best Practices

If a company wants to enforce the use of a set of best practices, it needs to link the existing set of company payroll policies to those best practices. By doing so, senior management is stating that it supports the improvements. This list of policies matches specific best practices noted earlier in this book, sorted by chapter:

- Chapter 2: Employee Time Tracking
  - *Employees can carry a maximum of __ hours of unused vacation time forward into the next calendar year.* This policy supports best practice 2.4, where the payroll department avoids tracking vacation time through the use of an honor system. A control over this approach is to cap carry-forward vacation time, so that someone abusing the honor system cannot do so to a significant extent.

- Chapter 3: Employee Benefits and Deductions
  - *The company does not make purchases on behalf of employees.* This policy supports best practice 3.1, where the payroll department avoids making a series of deductions from employee paychecks to pay itself back for a purchase made by the company on behalf of employees.
  - *It is not company policy to issue advances on employee pay.* This policy supports best practice 3.2, where the payroll department avoids making paycheck prepayments to employees in order to avoid a number of transaction steps.
  - *Group term life insurance shall match employee annual pay, up to the current IRS exclusion limit.* This policy supports best practice 3.4, where the payroll department avoids making a series of calculations to determine the excess value of group term life insurance coverage given to employees over the IRS exclusion limit, which is currently $50,000.
  - *Employees are eligible to participate in the corporate 401(k) plan as of their hiring date as full-time employees.* This policy supports best practice 3.10, where new employees are allowed to participate in the pension plan at once as part of the initial hiring process.
- Chapter 4: Payroll Forms and Reports
  - *The company will provide access to computer kiosks for all employees.* This policy supports best practice 4.4, where the company issues electronic W-2 forms to employees. Because government regulations require that employees give their approval to receive W-2 forms electronically, giving them access to computer equipment is a good way to improve the proportion of electronic W-2 forms issued.
- Chapter 5: Payments to Employees
  - *All employees shall be paid by direct deposit or payroll cards.* This policy supports best practices 5.1, 5.3, and 5.4, all of which involve electronic payments. This policy is better than one requiring only direct deposit payments, because the use of payroll cards also allows for electronic payments to any employees not having bank accounts.
  - *The payroll department will coordinate all employee incentive and reimbursement plans.* This policy supports best practices 5.6 and 5.7, which require the use of debit cards for incentive and reimbursement plans. By requiring centralization of these activities through the

payroll department, it is easier to determine the extent of any reportable income to employees.

- Chapter 6: Commission Calculations and Payments

  - *The commission calculation system shall not be altered without approval by the chief executive officer.* This policy supports best practice 6.1, where the commission plan is simplified in order to reduce the amount of pay calculations required by the payroll staff. By requiring high-level approval to make plan alterations, there is less chance that the sales manager will increase the plan's complexity gradually over time.

  - *Commissions shall be paid based only on cash received.* This policy supports best practice 6.6, which supports invoice collection efforts by giving the sales staff a considerable interest in receiving payment for invoices. This approach avoids the use of commission payments based solely on invoiced amounts.

  - *Final commissions for terminated sales staff shall be based on cash received from shipments made up until the termination date.* This policy supports best practice 6.7, which delays final commission payments until actual shipment data is available on which to make accurate commission calculations.

- Chapter 8: Payroll Management

  - At least ___% of the scoring for employee performance reviews shall be based on the completion of training, cross-training, and certification programs. This policy supports best practices 8.3, 8.4, and 8.5, which involve the creation of payroll training and certification programs.

  - *The chief financial officer must approve all off-cycle payrolls.* This policy supports best practice 8.11, which minimizes time-consuming off-cycle payrolls, by requiring such senior-level approval that most requestors will elect not to do so.

  - *The company shall conduct an annual pay structure review, with the goal of simplifying the pay structure.* This policy supports best practice 8.14, to simplify the pay structure, thereby reducing the effort required to calculate payments to employees.

  - *Service-level agreements (SLAs) shall be completed as part of the annual budgeting process.* This policy supports best practice 8.24, which requires the payroll department to conclude SLAs with other departments. By linking the budget to the SLAs, the payroll manager should have sufficient funding to comply with service commitments.

- Chapter 10: Payroll Controls
  - *Employees are responsible for removing ineligible family members from the company health plan.* This policy supports best practice 10.14, where the company periodically reviews participant status in the corporate medical plan. The policy places responsibility squarely on employees, so the company has the right to extract reimbursement from employees if they were incorrectly placing ineligible family members on their insurance applications.

12.2 Timekeeping Procedure in a Best Practices Environment

In a traditional timekeeping system, employees working in a single location use a time clock to punch their hours onto cards, while off-site employees fill out time sheets by hand and either fax or mail them to the payroll department. The payroll staff reviews both sets of information for missing data or errors (of which there tend to be quite a lot) and works with department managers and employees to fix the information. Several iterations can occur before all the data are complete. The payroll staff then has managers approve the submitted time information, which may include approvals for overtime, shift differentials, and excess levels of vacation or sick time taken. Finally, all this information must be summarized into pay categories by employee (e.g., 12 hours of overtime and 40 hours of regular time for John Smith) before being given to the payroll clerk in charge of manually entering this information into the payroll processing system. The general process flow for the traditional timekeeping procedure is shown in Exhibit 12.1.

The traditional timekeeping system is lengthy, subject to multiple iterations, and can yield a large number of errors despite the best efforts of the payroll staff. However, by using a number of best practices, the system can be altered so substantially that few of the original steps remain in the revised procedure shown in Exhibit 12.2.

Exhibit 12.1   Traditional Timekeeping Procedure Flowchart

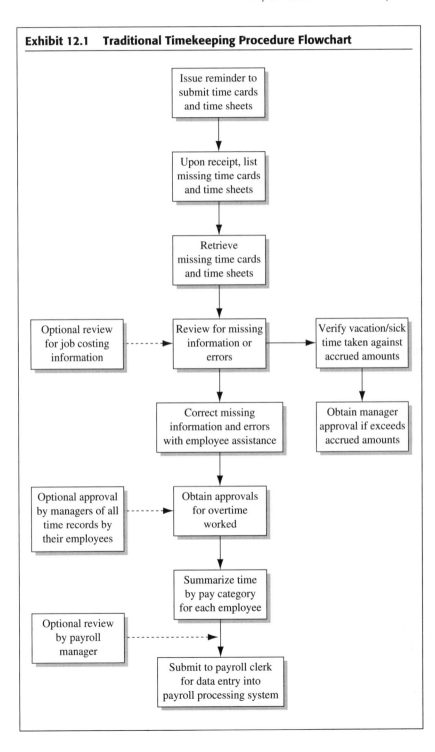

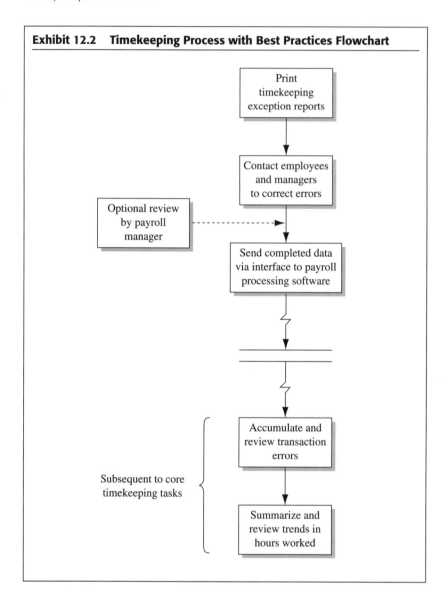

Exhibit 12.2   Timekeeping Process with Best Practices Flowchart

By using automated timekeeping systems, eliminating job costing through the payroll system, and using an honor system for vacation and sick time tracking, nearly all of the manual processing steps in the timekeeping procedure were avoided. The best practices noted in Exhibit 12.3, including their chapter reference number, were used to create this more streamlined approach.

Exhibit 12.3   Best Practices Used to Improve the Timekeeping Procedure

Best Practice Number	Description	Role in Procedure Improvement
2.7	Use bar-coded time clocks	Primary
2.9	Install a Web-based timekeeping system	Primary
2.10	Install automated time sheet reminders	Primary
2.5	Avoid job costing through the payroll system	Primary
2.4	Use honor system to track vacation and sick time	Primary
2.1	Switch to salaried positions	Secondary
2.2	Reduce the number of pay codes	Secondary
2.3	Eliminate personal leave days	Secondary
2.6	Use exception time reporting	Secondary
2.11	Track time with mobile phones	Secondary

Most of the best practices itemized as being of secondary importance in Exhibit 12.3 will reduce the volume of timekeeping transactions, but they will not automate the process. The single most important factor is to install an automated time clock or Web-based timekeeping system (or both), which handles most of the timekeeping chores.

The result of converting the revised timekeeping flowchart into a written procedure is shown in Exhibit 12.4.

In the procedure shown in Exhibit 12.4, there are two key items to be aware of. Note first that just two payroll clerks are involved. Due to process centering, just one person is responsible for all timekeeping reconciliation tasks. A second clerk fulfills the role of reviewing the results of the payroll. It would not be appropriate to assign the second clerk's role to the first clerk, because then the first clerk would be issuing reports about the quality of his or her own work, which is a conflict of interest.

The second item to note is the core dependence of this procedure on an automated timekeeping system. The payroll clerk merely ensures that the automated system is working with a complete set of current-employee information and then sorts through the automated error report to see what fixes are required. Virtually no manual collection or summarization of labor information is involved; instead, the payroll staff is placed in a review and analysis mode.

Exhibit 12.4   Revised Timekeeping Flowchart Converted to a Procedure

Policy/Procedure Statement	Retrieval No.:	PAY-01
	Page:	1 of 1
	Issue Date:	10/28/06
	Supercedes:	N/A

Subject: Timekeeping

1.   PURPOSE AND SCOPE

This procedure is used by the payroll department to collect and summarize employee hours worked.

2.   RESPONSIBILITIES

PAYCLERK1   **Payroll Clerk 1**
PAYCLERK2   **Payroll Clerk 2**

3.   PROCEDURES

3.1   PAYCLERK1   **Review Exception Reports**

1. Compare the current employee list to the list stored in the automated timekeeping system to verify that all current employees are included and that terminated employees have been removed.

2. If this is not the case, add new employees and delete terminated ones from the timekeeping system.

3. Print exception reports from the timekeeping system that address incomplete time punches or no time punches.

4. Highlight on the reports all items requiring adjustment prior to the next payroll run.

3.2   PAYCLERK1   **Correct Errors**

1. Contact each person on the highlighted report and collect from them all corrections needed.

2. Review corrections with supervisors to obtain their approval.

3. Enter the timekeeping system in supervisory mode and make the correcting entries for all employees in one batch.

4. Reprint the error reports to verify that all adjustments have been made correctly. If not, correct the adjustments and run the reports again.

Exhibit 12.4   (Continued)

3.3 PAYCLERK1   **Send Data to Payroll System**

1. In the timekeeping system, go to the data transmission interface and press the data transfer button to send the timekeeping data to the timekeeping system.

2. Contact the clerk in charge of payroll processing and verify that all data were received.

3.4 PAYCLERK2   **Accumulate and Review Transaction Errors**

1. Several days after payroll has been processed and paid, go to the pending payroll transactions folder and make copies of all adjusting entries stored there that relate to errors made during the last payroll cycle.

2. Examine entries made into the payroll system subsequent to the last payroll cycle and note the details of all transactions that are corrections of entries in previous cycles.

3. Summarize these data into a report showing a trend line of error types and the detail on each error transaction.

4. Present the report at the monthly payroll department error review meeting.

3.5 PAYCLERK2   **Summarize and Review Trends in Hours Worked**

1. Print from the timekeeping system a listing of hours worked by pay category.

2. Add this information to an electronic spreadsheet report that stores the data on a trend line.

3. If there are significant changes in the trend line, investigate the reasons for the changes. Note these reasons in an accompanying report.

4. Issue the summary and review in a report to the payroll manager as well as the financial analyst in the accounting department.

12.3 Payroll Processing Procedure in a Best Practices Environment

Processing payroll is similar to pushing a large quantity of water through a small hole—there is a serious data-entry bottleneck for the payroll staff. When processing time arrives, the payroll staff faces a large heap of change requests to process, which include garnishments, tax deductions, direct deposit changes, pension plan deductions, shift differentials, terminations, new hires, bonuses, commissions, and benefits deductions—not to mention the timekeeping information from the preceding procedure that must now be entered into the system. There is no particular order or flow to the arrival of this information, so the payroll staff deals with different types of information in a jumbled order. There are also likely to be some iterations of the payroll processing due to error corrections, given the large amount of data entry being completed. The result is shown in Exhibit 12.5.

A comprehensive revamping of the payroll processing routine results in an entirely different process flow, as shown in Exhibit 12.6. Under this newer approach, employee self-service has resulted in all employee-initiated payroll changes being shifted back onto the shoulders of the employees, including all changes to addresses, tax deductions, direct deposit information, pension plan deductions, and benefits deductions. Further, the use of manager self-service shifts all remaining change information to the various supervisors throughout the company, while a data interface automatically pulls in all timekeeping information from the timekeeping system. As a result, the payroll staff is taken out of the data-entry business, instead spending its time reviewing incoming data for errors and making revisions only on an exception basis.

The best practices noted in Exhibit 12.7, including their best practice reference number, were used to create this more streamlined approach. Most of the best practices itemized in the exhibit as being of secondary importance are designed to reduce the volume of deductions in the payroll system or to smooth out the flow of work within the department, but they will not help to automate the overall system further.

The result of converting the revised payroll processing flowchart into a written procedure is shown in Exhibit 12.8.

Exhibit 12.5   Traditional Payroll Processing Procedure Flowchart

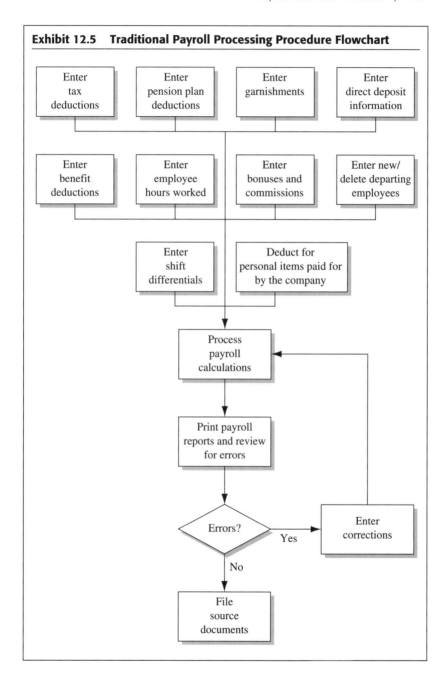

Exhibit 12.6 Payroll Processing with Best Practices Flowchart

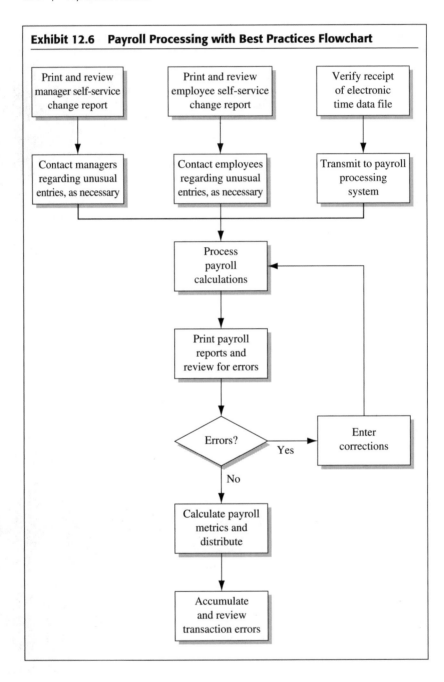

Exhibit 12.7   Best Practices Used to Improve the Payroll Processing Procedure

Best Practice Number	Description	Role in Procedure Improvement
7.1	Outsource the payroll function	Primary
8.10	Minimize payroll cycles	Primary
3.13	Create employee self-service for payroll changes	Primary
8.20	Install manager self-service	Primary
8.11	Minimize off-cycle payrolls	Secondary
10.11	Verify that the payroll database has been updated with all manual checks	Secondary
3.1	Prohibit deductions for employee purchases	Secondary
3.2	Disallow prepayments	Secondary
3.3	Minimize payroll deductions	Secondary
3.4	Cap group term life insurance at the IRS exclusion limit	Secondary
3.6	Isolate in-pats and ex-pats in separate pay groups	Secondary
5.12	Charge intercompany fees for manual paychecks	Secondary
8.8	Process non pay-affecting changes during off-peak periods	Secondary
8.9	Implement process centering	Secondary

Exhibit 12.8   Revised Payroll Processing Flowchart Converted to a Procedure

Policy/Procedure Statement	Retrieval No.:	PAY-02
	Page:	1 of 1
	Issue Date:	10/28/06
	Supercedes:	N/A

Subject: Payroll Processing

1. PURPOSE AND SCOPE

This procedure is used by the payroll department to calculate payments due to employees.

(*continues*)

Exhibit 12.8   (Continued)

2. RESPONSIBILITIES

PAYCLERK1	**Payroll Clerk 1**
PAYCLERK2	**Payroll Clerk 2**

3. PROCEDURES

3.1 PAYCLERK1   **Review Self-Service Information**

1. Print and review the self-service change reports generated by the manager and employee payroll self-service systems.

2. Contact managers or employees regarding any unusual entries or entries that exceed policy limits.

3.2 PAYCLERK1   **Import Timekeeping Information**

1. Upon notification from the payroll clerk responsible for timekeeping, import the timekeeping data file through the automated interface.

2. Verify that the file has been received without errors.

3.3 PAYCLERK1   **Process Payroll Calculations**

1. Run the payroll calculations for this payroll cycle in the payroll software.

2. Print the transaction register and review it for errors.

3. If there are errors, make corrections and run the payroll calculations again.

4. Once errors are expunged from the payroll cycle, notify the payroll clerk in charge of payroll payments that the payroll information is ready for processing.

3.4 PAYCLERK2   **Calculate Payroll Metrics**

1. Print from the payroll system a summary of all gross pay, deductions, and net pay by department.

2. Add this information to an electronic spreadsheet report that stores the data on a trend line.

3. If there are significant changes in the trend line, investigate the reasons for the changes. Note these reasons in an accompanying report.

4. Issue the summary and review in a report to the payroll manager as well as the financial analyst in the accounting department.

Exhibit 12.8   (Continued)

3.5 PAYCLERK2   **Accumulate and Review Transaction Errors**

1. Several days after payroll has been processed, go to the pending payroll transactions folder and make copies of all adjusting entries stored there that relate to errors made during the last payroll cycle.

2. Examine entries made into the payroll system subsequent to the last payroll cycle and note the details of all transactions that are corrections of entries in previous cycles.

3. Summarize these data into a report showing a trend line of error types and the detail of each error transaction.

4. Present the report at the monthly payroll department error review meeting.

In the procedure, note the minimal amount of data entry required—just to correct errors that crop up after the payroll has been processed initially. Otherwise, the high level of automation shifts the data-entry burden over to department managers and employees, while the payroll clerks spend their time looking for exceptions. Also, a second payroll clerk is used to calculate performance metrics; by doing so, the clerk responsible for payroll processing is not also reporting on his or her own performance. Finally, it is critical to track transaction errors through such a highly automated system, because the systems development staff needs to know what problems keep recurring; the staff can use this information to design into the self-service computer interfaces fail-safe features that will mitigate these problems.

12.4 Payment Distribution Procedure in a Best Practices Environment

Consider a lengthy and tightly controlled check-printing procedure in a traditional payroll payment distribution environment: the payroll clerk removes check stock and a signature plate from the company safe, obtains access to the password-protected computer to which the payroll printer is attached, and prints paychecks from that location. Then the clerk prints a check register, logs in the range of check numbers used, and returns the signature plate and all remaining check stock to the safe. Next, the clerk stuffs all the paychecks into envelopes and hands them over to a paymaster, who personally distributes them to employees. If any checks go unclaimed, the paymaster records these checks and stores them in the safe. This process flow is shown in Exhibit 12.9.

Although printing checks is not a terribly difficult procedure for the payroll staff, it is easier to distribute funds electronically, using the revised procedure shown in Exhibit 12.10. Under this approach, direct deposit becomes the dominant form of payment. If the department has attempted a prenotification to verify a bank's routing and account number and the prenotification failed, then the traditional check-printing process must be followed. Otherwise, the payroll clerk stores the direct deposit information in a file and electronically ships it off to the company bank, which handles the direct deposit transaction on behalf of the company. The same file or a similar one containing additional pay and deduction information also can be used to load the corporate electronic pay stub system, so that employees can access their payroll remittance advices over the Internet. Alternatively, this information can be sent to a third party that handles electronic distribution to employees.

The best practices noted in Exhibit 12.11, including their best practice reference number, were used to create this more streamlined approach. A number of the best practices itemized as being of secondary importance in the exhibit are designed to force employees to use direct deposit or make the payment process flow more smoothly.

The result of converting the revised payment distribution flowchart into a written procedure is shown in Exhibit 12.12.

Exhibit 12.9   Traditional Payment Distribution Procedure Flowchart

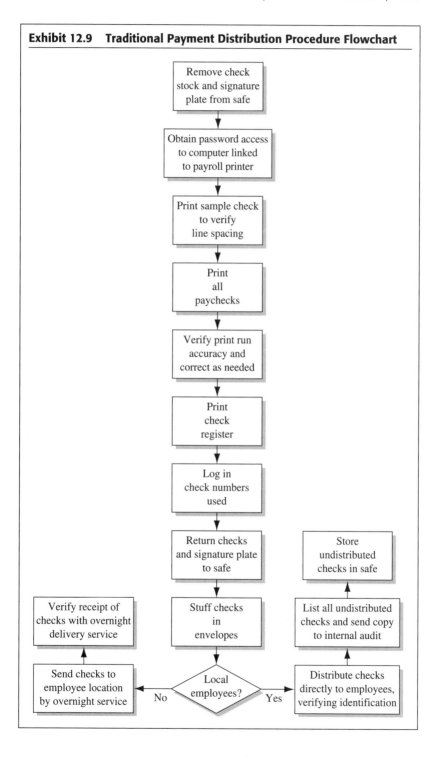

Exhibit 12.10   Payment Distribution with Best Practices Flowchart

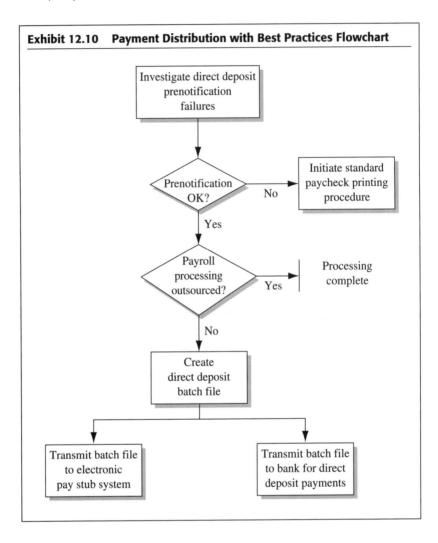

Exhibit 12.11 Best Practices Used to Improve the Payment Distribution Procedure

Best Practice Number	Description	Role in Procedure Improvement
5.1	Use direct deposit	Primary
5.3	Pay employees through payroll cards	Primary
5.9	Post payroll remittances on company intranet	Primary
7.4	Outsource tax filings	Primary
10.6	Initiate direct deposit prenotifications	Secondary
5.2	Stop delivering checks to employees at the office	Secondary
5.4	Offer clear cards to employees	Secondary
5.10	Allow online payroll remittance viewing only if employees use direct deposit	Secondary
5.8	Send payroll remittances by e-mail	Secondary
8.19	Make electronic child support garnishment payments	Secondary

Exhibit 12.12 Revised Payment Distribution Flowchart Converted to a Procedure

Policy/Procedure Statement	Retrieval No.:	PAY-03
	Page:	1 of 1
	Issue Date:	10/28/06
	Supercedes:	N/A

Subject: Payment Distribution

1. **PURPOSE AND SCOPE**

   This procedure is used by the payroll department to issue payments to employees.

2. **RESPONSIBILITIES**

   PAYCLERK1   **Payroll Clerk 1**

   (*continues*)

Exhibit 12.12   (Continued)

---

3.   PROCEDURES

3.1 PAYCLERK 1   **Investigate Prenotification Failures**

1. Obtain direct deposit prenotification failure messages from the bank.

2. Contact all employees for whom these failures occurred, and request a copy of a voided check drawn on their deposit accounts.

3. Once received, verify the ABA and account numbers on the checks and resubmit prenotification transactions to the bank.

4. Enter the employee numbers for all employees having prenotification failures into the payroll system, so they will be issued regular paychecks through the standard paycheck printing process.

5. Print a report listing the employee numbers and names of these employees.

3.2 PYCLERK 1   **Create Direct Deposit Batch File**

1. Create the direct deposit batch file using the payroll software.

2. Print the batch file report and compare it to the prenotification failure report to ensure that no employees are listed on both reports.

3. Electronically transmit the file to the bank handling direct deposit transfers.

4. Transmit the file to the company's electronic payroll remittance advice system. If this system requires additional information regarding employee tax or other data, create a separate file from the payroll software and transmit this file instead.

13

Best Practices Implementation Plan

There are over 120 payroll best practices in this book. Which one comes first? Many readers will jump straight to the Appendix to peruse the list of best practices and will pick those appearing to represent the easiest fixes. Once they install those best practices, they will return to the Appendix and pick a few more. Although this approach eventually will result in a more efficient payroll department, readers may never select those few best practices representing quantum leaps forward in overall payroll efficiency. This chapter is intended to direct readers to specific subsets of best practices that will result in the greatest possible improvements.

13.1 Improve Payroll Management

The first improvement step is to be absolutely sure of how the payroll department already operates, as it is difficult to lead an implementation effort when one does not know what impact a new best practice will have on the department. Consequently, the first action item is to construct a policies and procedures manual (best practice 8.1). The mere effort of documenting department processes will yield a considerable return to the payroll manager, who may not be aware of the subtleties of various processes. Next, this information should be converted into a set of activity calendars for each employee (best practice 8.2), which yields a more detailed view of the workload of everyone within the department. The final action is to construct a method for accumulating and summarizing the various types of transaction errors occurring within the department (best practice 8.6). This information provides evidence of where the department's procedures and training programs are falling short.

Note that the only management-related recommendations being made are *exploratory* in nature—they are designed to document the current process *only*. They do not attempt to make any stopgap improvements to the system, because it is easier to wait until other core processes have been replaced and then return to the management function and make additional changes at that time. For example, it is not useful to implement an employee training program yet, because training would involve procedures that are likely to change in the near future.

13.2 Reduce Transaction Volume

The payroll manager may try to implement a series of best practices at this point, but staff members may push back by saying that they are completely overworked and have no time to make any changes. If so, one can consider a series of steps designed to reduce the department workload. If there is a significant backlog of transactions to be entered, one can consider bringing in experienced part-time staff to clear out the excess transactions (best practice 8.7) and schedule them to return for as many payroll cycles as needed until other best practices eliminate the backlog. Next, it is useful to gain senior management support to reduce the number of off-cycle payrolls (best practice 8.11), eliminate reports (best practice 4.1), disallow payroll advances (best practice 3.2), prohibit deductions for employee purchases (best practice 3.1), and avoid job costing through the payroll system (best practice 2.5). Although a number of these changes will meet with resistance from outside the department, it should be possible to implement a sufficient number to make a small positive impact on the department workload. A larger change that requires more time to implement, but that has a correspondingly greater impact on workload reduction, is to reduce the number of payroll cycles (best practice 8.10). By making as many of these changes as possible, the department should have sufficient time available to implement more significant best practices.

13.3 Automate Timekeeping

Accumulating hours worked is one of the most labor-intensive tasks faced by the payroll department. It is also rife with errors, which causes considerable employee dissatisfaction. For these reasons, it is an excellent choice for the first major set of best practice improvements. The single greatest improvement in this area is to install a set of computerized time clocks (best practices 2.7 and 2.8), which automatically spot timekeeping errors and take the payroll staff completely out of the data-entry business. If employees work in highly distributed locations, it may be necessary to install a Web-based timekeeping system (best practice 2.9) coupled with an automated time sheet reminder system (best practice 2.10). For traveling employees without access to computers, a third alternative is to track time worked with mobile phones (best practice 2.11). All of these systems still must deal with the ongoing problem of employees who persistently forget to log in their hours, which places the payroll staff in the annoying position of having to track them down. Consequently, it is extremely useful to convert as many employees as possible to exception-based time reporting (best practice 2.6), so fewer people must actively enter their hours into the system on an ongoing basis.

Once these changes have been implemented, it is useful to modify the procedures manual and employee activity calendars to reflect these changes. Also, one should consider setting up a training program (best practice 8.3) just for the timekeeping area; as the timekeeping function now can be expected to be stable for some time, it is economical to invest some effort in constructing a short training module covering the area.

The exact configuration of the various timekeeping systems will depend on the distribution and types of employees within a company, but the main goal is simple enough: the payroll staff should not be keying time data into a computer system. Let the employees do that instead.

13.4 Implement Self-Service

Processing the large number of deductions, information changes, and timekeeping entries required for each payroll cycle can be a monumental chore, especially when there are a large number of employees who are all paid on the same payroll cycle. The payroll manager should not be in the data-entry business, and the way to get out of it is to implement employee and manager self-service. To do so, the first step is to hand over the payroll processing function to a payroll outsourcing company (best practices 7.1 and 7.2). A number of payroll suppliers now offer a Web-based self-service function (best practice 3.13), which is otherwise an expensive custom development project to create. However, no payroll suppliers currently offer manager self-service as well, so the outsourcing option still will require some data entry by the payroll staff for such items as pay raises and bonuses. If using manager self-service is critical, then the payroll manager can sponsor the development of an in-house manager self-service system (best practice 3.14) and then upload the data to the outsourced payroll system, or else keep the entire payroll processing function in-house and develop all self-service functions internally.

Once these changes are installed, it is again time to update the procedures manual and training program to reflect all changes made to the payroll system.

13.5 Make Electronic Payments

At this point, the payroll department will have been largely removed from the data-entry business, but it still must deal with the lesser problem of printing paychecks and distributing them. The solution is to switch the workforce over to electronic payments by requiring either direct deposit (best practice 5.1) or payments through payroll cards (best practice 5.3) for those employees without bank accounts. However, these two steps do not eliminate the distribution of remittance advices (pay stubs), so it is also necessary to either e-mail this information to employees (best practice 5.8) or, more commonly, post it to a Web site where they can access it (best practice 5.9). A final refinement is also to issue W-2 forms electronically (best practice 4.4). By taking these steps, there is no need to issue paychecks to employees, unless they are new employees who are not yet set up for electronic payments.

After implementing the changes in this section, it is again time to update the procedures manual and training program.

13.6 Install Metrics

At this point, the payroll department's operations will have been upgraded significantly, and it is time to ensure that there is no increase in error rates or drop in departmental efficiency. Doing this calls for the installation of a select few metrics, which will vary by company circumstances. The payroll transaction error rate (best practice 11.2) certainly should be installed in any payroll department, thereby focusing staff attention on error reduction. Also, the proportion of payroll entries to headcount (best practice 11.4) is a good indicator of the department's ability to simplify the deduction structure. In both cases, one tracks the measurements on a trend line covering at least the past year and also reports on the underlying information in sufficient detail to show payroll employees precisely what areas must be fixed.

13.7 Ensure Ongoing Improvements

Although now the payroll department has installed the core best practices and finds itself in the enjoyable position of simply monitoring pay information entered by other people in the company, there is always room for improvement. Also, a basic rule of system complexity is that any system will begin to degrade as soon as the company stops trying to improve it. For both of these reasons, the payroll manager must insist on several additional steps to ensure that systems continue to improve. One task is to implement cross-training within the department (best practice 8.4), which not only gives everyone the training to back each other up on critical tasks, but also gives all payroll staff members a better knowledge of the entire department's operations, so they are in a better position to suggest improvements throughout the system. Another task is to require as many of the payroll staff members as possible to obtain a payroll certification (best practice 8.5). The extra level of knowledge obtained through the certification process is also helpful for making further system improvements. Also, one must keep digging for errors (best practices 8.6 and 10.7), because these are evidence of system problems; by fixing what caused the errors to occur, the overall payroll system will continue to improve. Finally, one should consider using process centering (best practice 8.9), which fosters the mind-set of constantly reviewing processes to see how they can be simplified. The combination of all these actions will result in a payroll staff that is vigilant in looking for ways to improve the department.

13.8 Summary

This chapter was intended to bring some order to the large cluster of best practices presented throughout this book by focusing the reader's attention on the roughly 20% that can yield the most significant results. However, this only presents a certain path to follow that may not correlate to the specific problems that a company faces. For example, a payroll manager may have just discovered a large-scale case of payment fraud within the department, and so feels compelled to jump straight into the installation of electronic payment systems, bypassing all other improvements until this control problem is fixed.

However, no matter what order of implementation the payroll manager chooses to follow, there is one important lesson to be learned from this chapter: It is better to install a set of best practices in one functional area rather than to make a number of small unrelated improvements. By clustering the work effort into a single area, best practices tend to support each other to create greater efficiencies than would otherwise be the case. For example, installing a computerized timekeeping system will result in improvements, but if the payroll staff still must conduct time data entry for off-site employees, then the department has not truly divorced itself from the data-entry function. Instead, a comprehensive and interlocking set of computerized timekeeping systems must be installed, so that payroll employees can fully realize the benefits of timekeeping computerization.

Finally, no matter what approach one decides to take in implementing payroll best practices, it is important to create and follow an implementation plan to reach whatever goal is set. By using this chapter as the basis for setting up and following a custom-tailored plan, including resource requirements and a timeline, the payroll manager will have a much better chance of eventually arriving at the goal of a modern, highly efficient payroll department.

Payroll Best Practices Summary

This appendix includes the title and reference number for every best practice listed in the book and serves as a quick reference guide. In addition, the formulas for all the measurements noted in Chapter 11 are listed at the end of the appendix.

Chapter 2: Employee Time Tracking

2.1   Switch to salaried positions

2.2   Reduce the number of pay codes

2.3   Eliminate personal leave days

2.4   Use honor system to track vacation and sick time

2.5   Avoid job costing through the payroll system

2.6   Use exception time reporting

2.7   Use bar-coded time clocks

2.8   Use biometric time clocks

2.9   Install a Web-based timekeeping system

2.10   Install automated time sheet reminders

2.11   Track time with mobile phones

Chapter 3: Employee Benefits and Deductions

3.1   Prohibit deductions for employee purchases

3.2   Disallow prepayments

3.3   Minimize payroll deductions

3.4   Cap group term life insurance coverage at the IRS exclusion limit

3.5   Charge employees a fee for garnishment processing

Chapter 4:   Payroll Forms and Reports

Chapter 5:   Payments to Employees

5.11   Install ATMs at company locations

5.12   Charge intercompany fees for manual paychecks

5.13   Use automated folders and sealers for paychecks

5.14   Use IRS letter-forwarding service to deliver unclaimed paychecks

Chapter 6:   Commission Calculations and Payments

6.1   Simplify the commission structure

6.2   Construct a standard commission terms table

6.3   Periodically issue a summary of commission rates

6.4   Calculate commissions automatically in the computer system

6.5   Install incentive compensation management software

6.6   Pay commissions only from cash received

6.7   Calculate final commissions from actual data

6.8   Include commission payments in payroll payments

6.9   Lengthen the interval between commission payments

6.10   Periodically audit commissions paid

6.11   Post commission payments on the company intranet

6.12   Avoid adjusting preliminary commission accrual calculations

Chapter 7:   Payroll Outsourcing

7.1   Outsource the payroll function

7.2   Use Web-based payroll outsourcing

7.3   Outsource benefits administration to a payroll supplier

7.4   Outsource tax filings

7.5   Outsource W-2 form creation and delivery

7.6   Link hosted payroll processing to an ERP system

7.7   Outsource unemployment claims management

Chapter 8:   Payroll Management

Basic Department Management

8.1   Create a policies and procedures manual

8.2   Issue activity calendars to all payroll employees

8.3   Create a payroll training program

Chapter 9: Payroll Systems

9.1   Consolidate payroll systems

9.2   Install an integrated human resources and payroll system

9.3   Install an enterprise workforce management system

9.4   Install a work-flow management system

9.5   Implement document imaging

9.6   Install a data warehouse

9.7   Use a forms/rates data warehouse for automated tax filings

9.8   Avoid legacy payroll systems

Chapter 10: Payroll Controls

10.1   Create a backup system for payroll records

10.2   Isolate access to the payroll check-printing capability

10.3   Scan fingerprints at user workstations

10.4   Incorporate copy protection features into checks

10.5   Implement positive pay

10.6   Initiate direct deposit prenotifications

10.7   Create standard error-checking reports

10.8   Review payroll trends after each pay run

10.9   Create standard payroll audit reports

10.10   Reconcile the payroll bank account every day with online Internet access

10.11   Verify that the payroll database has been updated with all manual checks

10.12   Verify amounts owed by employees at termination

10.13   Verify that year-end paid leave balances are accrued and carried forward properly

10.14   Review insurance for presence of ineligible family members

Chapter 11: Payroll Measurements

11.1 $$\frac{\text{Total payroll outsourcing fee per payroll}}{\text{Total number of employees itemized in payroll}}$$

11.2 $$\frac{\text{Number of payroll transaction errors}}{\text{Total number of payroll entries}}$$

11.3 $$\frac{\text{Total number of W-2c forms issued}}{\text{Total number of W-2 forms issued}}$$

11.4 $$\frac{\text{Total deductions} + \text{Total memo entries} + \text{Total goal entries}}{\text{Total number of full-time equivalents}}$$

11.5

$$\frac{\text{Fixed base pay} + \text{Wages} + \text{Commissions} + \text{Overtime} + \text{Bonuses} + \text{Total other variable pay}}{\text{Total number of full-time equivalents}}$$

11.6 $$\frac{\text{Total cost of time off} + \text{Insurance} + \text{Other benefits} - \text{Employee deductions}}{\text{Total number of full-time equivalents}}$$

11.7 $$\frac{\text{Annualized revenue}}{\text{Total full-time equivalents}}$$

Glossary[*]

401(k) Plan. A retirement plan set up by an employer, into which employees can contribute the lesser of $13,000 or 15% of their pay (as of 2004), which is excluded from taxation until such time as they remove the funds from the account.

403(b) Plan. A retirement plan similar to a 401(k) plan, except that it is designed specifically for charitable, religious, and education organizations that fall under the tax-exempt status of 501(c)(3) regulations.

ABC Test. A test used to determine the status of an employee under a state unemployment insurance program, where a person is a contractor only if there is an *a*bsence of control by the company, *b*usiness conducted by the employee is substantially different from that of the company, and the person *c*ustomarily works independently from the company.

Alien. The citizen of a country other than the United States.

Automated Clearing House (ACH). A banking clearinghouse that processes direct deposit transfers.

Benefit Ratio Method. The proportion of unemployment benefits paid to a company's former employees during the measurement period, divided by the total payroll during the period. This calculation is used by states to determine the unemployment contribution rate to charge employers.

Benefit Wage Ratio Method. The proportion of total taxable wages for laid off employees during the measurement period, divided by the total payroll during the period. This calculation is used by states to determine the unemployment contribution rate to charge employers.

---

[*]Adapted with permission from Steven M. Bragg, *Accounting for Payroll* (Hoboken, NJ: John Wiley & Sons, 2004), Appendix B.

Cafeteria Plan. A flexible benefits plan authorized under the Internal Revenue Code, allowing employees to pay for a selection of benefits with pay deductions, some of which may be pretax.

Clear Card. A credit card from which payments are deducted over subsequent time periods.

Compensation. All forms of pay given to an employee in exchange for services rendered.

Consolidated Omnibus Budget Reconciliation Act (COBRA). A federal act containing the requirements for offering insurance to departed employees.

Consumer Credit Protection Act. A federal act specifying the proportion of total pay that may be garnished.

Contract Work Hours and Safety Standards Act. A federal act requiring federal contractors to pay overtime for hours worked exceeding 40 per week.

Contribution Rate. The percentage tax charged by a state to an employer to cover its share of the state unemployment insurance fund.

Coverdell Education IRA. A form of individual retirement account whose earnings during the period when funds are stored in the IRA will be tax-free at the time when they are used to pay for the cost of advanced education.

Current Tax Payment Act of 1943. A federal act requiring employers to withhold income taxes from employee pay.

Davis-Bacon Act of 1931. A federal act providing wage protection to non-government workers by requiring businesses engaged in federal construction projects to pay their employees prevailing wages and fringe benefits.

Defined Benefit Plan. A pension plan that pays out a predetermined dollar amount to participants, based on a set of rules that typically combine the number of years of employment and wages paid over the time period when each employee worked for the company.

Defined Contribution Plan. A qualified retirement plan under which the employer is liable for a payment into the plan of a specific size, but not for the size of the resulting payments from the plan to participants.

Direct Deposit. The direct transfer of payroll funds from the company bank account directly into that of the employee, avoiding the use of a paycheck.

Educational Assistance Plan. A plan that an employer creates on behalf of its employees, covering a variety of educational expenses incurred on behalf of employees, for which they can avoid recognizing some income.

Electronic Federal Tax Payment Systems (EFTPS). An electronic funds transfer system used by businesses to remit taxes to the government.

Employee. A person who renders services to another entity in exchange for compensation.

Employee Retirement Income Security Act of 1974 (ERISA). A federal act that sets minimum operational and funding standards for employee benefit plans.

Employee Stock Ownership Plan (ESOP). A fund containing company stock and owned by employees, paid for by ongoing contributions by the employer.

Employer. A person or entity that directs and controls the work of individuals in exchange for compensation.

Equal Pay Act of 1963. A federal act requiring that both sexes receive equal pay in situations where work requires equivalent effort, responsibility, and skills, performed under similar working conditions.

Escalating Price Option. A nonqualified stock option that uses a sliding scale for the option price that changes in concert with a peer group index.

Fair Labor Standards Act of 1938. A federal act creating standards of overtime pay, minimum wages, and payroll record keeping.

Family and Medical Leave Act. A federal act containing the rules for offering health insurance to employees who are on leave.

Federal Employer Identification Number. A unique identification number issued by the federal government, used for payroll purposes to identify the company when it deals with the Internal Revenue Service.

Federal Insurance Contributions Act of 1935 (FICA). A federal act authorizing the government to collect social security and Medicare payroll taxes.

Federal Unemployment Tax Act (FUTA). A federal act requiring employers to pay a tax on the wages paid to their employees, which is then used to create a pool of funds to be used for unemployment benefits.

FICA. The acronym for the Federal Insurance Contributions Act, also used to describe the combined amount of social security and Medicare deductions from an employee's pay.

Flexible Spending Account. A form of cafeteria plan, allowing employees to pay for some medical or dependent care expenses with pretax pay deductions.

Form 1099. A form used by businesses to report to the government payments made to certain types of suppliers.

Form 4070. A form used by employees to report to an employer the amount of their tip income.

Form 668-W. The standard form used for notifying a company to garnish an employee's wages for unpaid taxes.

Form 8027. The form used by employers to report tip income by their employees to the government.

Form 940. A form used to report federal unemployment tax remittances and liabilities.

Form 940-EZ. A shortened version of the Form 940.

Form 941. A form used to identify to the government the amount of all quarterly wages on which taxes were withheld, the amount of taxes withheld, and any adjustments to withheld taxes from previous reporting periods.

Form I-9. The Employment Eligibility Verification form, which must be filled out for all new employees, in which they establish their identity and eligibility to work.

Garnishment. A court-ordered authorization to shift employee wages to a creditor.

Green Card. The I-551 Permanent Resident Card, held by a resident alien.

Gross Pay. The amount of earnings due to an employee prior to tax and other deductions.

Health Insurance Portability and Accountability Act of 1996 (HIPAA). A federal act expanding on many of the insurance reforms created by COBRA. In particular, it ensures that small businesses will have access to health insurance, despite the special health status of any employees.

Heavenly Parachute Stock Option. A nonqualified stock option that allows a deceased option holder's estate up to three years in which to exercise his or her options.

Hourly Rate Plan. A method for calculating wages for hourly employees that involves the multiplication of the wage rate per hour times the number of hours worked during the workweek.

Illegal Immigration Reform and Immigrant Responsibility Act of 1996 (IIRIRA). A federal act shielding employers from liability if they have made a good-faith effort to verify a new employee's identity and employment eligibility.

Immigration Reform and Control Act of 1986. A federal act requiring all employers having at least four employees to verify the identity and employment eligibility of all regular, temporary, casual, and student employees.

Incentive Stock Option. An option to purchase company stock that is not taxable to the employee at the time it is granted, nor at the time when the employee eventually exercises the option to buy stock.

Individual Retirement Account (IRA). A personal savings account into which a defined maximum amount may be contributed, and for which any resulting interest is tax-deferred.

Individual Retirement Annuity. An IRA comprised of an annuity that is managed through and paid out by a life insurance company.

Internal Revenue Code. Refers to all federal tax laws as a group.

Internal Revenue Service (IRS). A federal agency empowered by Congress to interpret and enforce tax-related laws.

McNamara-O'Hara Service Contract Act of 1965. A federal act requiring federal contractors to pay those employees working on a federal contract at least as much as the wage and benefit levels prevailing locally.

Minimum Wage. An hourly wage rate set by the federal government below which actual hourly wages cannot fall. This rate can be increased by state governments.

Net Pay. The amount of an employee's wages payable after all tax and other deductions have been removed.

Non-Qualified Retirement Plan. A pension plan that does not follow ERISA and IRS guidelines, typically allowing a company to pay key personnel more than other participants.

Nonqualified Stock Option. A stock option not given any favorable tax treatment under the Internal Revenue Code. The option is taxed when it is exercised, based on the difference between the option price and the fair market value of the stock on that day.

Outsourcing. The process of shifting a function previously performed internally to a supplier that is responsible to the company for ongoing operations and results.

Overtime. A pay premium of 50% of the regular rate of pay that is earned by employees on all hours worked beyond 40 hours in a standard workweek.

Pay Card. A credit card into which a company directly deposits an employee's net pay.

Payroll Cycle. The period of service for which a company compensates its employees.

Payroll Register. A report on which is summarized the wage and deduction information for employees for a specific payroll.

Payroll Stabilization. A calculation used by states to determine the unemployment contribution rate to charge employers. It links the contribution rate to fluctuations in a company's total payroll over time.

Per Diem. A fixed rate paid to employees traveling on behalf of a business, which substitutes for reimbursement of exact expenses incurred.

Personal Responsibility and Work Opportunity Reconciliation Act. A federal act requiring the reporting of new hires into a national database.

Piece Rate Plan. A wage calculation method based on the number of units of production completed by an employee.

Premium Grant. A nonqualified stock option whose option price is set substantially higher than the current fair market value at the grant date.

Profit Sharing Plan. A retirement plan generally funded by a percentage of company profits, but into which contributions can be made in the absence of profits.

Qualified Retirement Plan. A retirement plan designed to observe all of the requirements of the Employee Retirement Income Security Act (ERISA), which allows an employer to immediately deduct allowable contributions to the plan on behalf of plan participants.

Reserve Ratio. A calculation used by states to determine the unemployment contribution rate to charge employers. The ongoing balance of a firm's unclaimed contributions from previous years is reduced by unemployment claims for the past year and then divided by the average annual payroll, resulting in a "reserve ratio."

Rollover IRA. An IRA that an individual sets up for the express purpose of receiving funds from a qualified retirement plan.

Roth IRA. An IRA account whose earnings are not taxable at all under certain circumstances.

Savings Incentive Match Plan for Employees (SIMPLE). An IRA set up by an employer with no other retirement plan and employing fewer than 100 employees, into which they can contribute up to $9,000 per year (as of 2004).

Section 83(b) Election. The decision by an employee to recognize taxable income on the purchase price of an incentive stock option within 30 days following the date when an option is exercised and to withhold taxes at the ordinary income tax rate at that time.

Self-Employment Contributions Act (SECA). A federal act requiring self-employed business owners to pay the same total tax rates for social security and Medicare taxes that are split between employees and employers under the Federal Insurance Contributions Act (FICA).

Sick Pay. A fixed amount of pay benefit available to employees who cannot work due to sickness. Company policy fixes the amount of this benefit that can be carried forward into future periods.

Signature Card. A bank document containing the signatures of all approved signatories that a company has approved to sign checks.

Signature Plate. A stamp on which is inscribed an authorized check signer's signature, and which is used to imprint the signature on completed checks.

Social Security Act of 1935. A federal Act establishing Old Age and Survivor's Insurance, which was funded by compulsory savings by wage earners.

State Disability Tax. A tax charged by selected states to maintain a disability insurance fund, from which payments are made to employees who are unable to work due to illness or injury.

Target Benefit Plan. A defined benefit plan under which the employer makes annual contributions into the plan based on the actuarial assumption at that time regarding the amount of funding needed to achieve a targeted benefit level.

Termination Pay. Additional pay due to an employ whose employment is being terminated, usually in accordance with a termination pay schedule contained within the employee manual.

Time Card. A document or electronic record on which an employee records his or her hours worked during a payroll period.

Time Clock. A device used to stamp an employee's incoming or outgoing time on either a paper document or an electronic record.

Totalization Agreement. An agreement between countries whereby an employee has to pay social security taxes only to the country in which he or she is working.

Unclaimed Pay. Net pay not collected by an employee, which typically is transferred to the local state government after a mandated interval has passed from the date of payment.

Uniform Interstate Family Support Act. A federal act specifying which jurisdiction shall issue family support-related garnishment orders.

Uniformed Services Employment and Reemployment Rights Act of 1994. A federal act that minimizes the impact on people serving in the armed forces when they return to civilian employment by avoiding discrimination and increasing their employment opportunities.

W-2 Form. A form used to report gross pay and tax deductions for each employee to the IRS for a calendar year.

W-4 Form. A form on which an employee declares the amount of federal tax deductions to be deducted from his or her pay.

W-9 Form. A form issued to a company's suppliers, requesting that they identify their form of legal organization and tax identification number.

Walsh-Healey Public Contracts Act of 1936. A federal act that forces government contractors to comply with the government's minimum wage and hour rules.

Workweek. A fixed period of 168 consecutive hours that recurs on a consistent basis.

Workers' Compensation Benefits. Employer-paid insurance that provides employees with wage compensation if they are injured on the job.

Index–Payroll Best Practices